State of the Union Addresses
of Franklin D. Roosevelt

by

Franklin D. Roosevelt

The Echo Library 2007

Published by

The Echo Library

Echo Library
131 High St.
Teddington
Middlesex TW11 8HH

www.echo-library.com

Please report serious faults in the text to complaints@echo-library.com

ISBN 978-1-40684-025-4

Dates of addresses by Franklin D. Roosevelt in this book:

January 3, 1934
January 7, 1943
January 11, 1944
January 6, 1945
January 4, 1935
January 3, 1936
January 6, 1937
January 3, 1938
January 4, 1939
January 3, 1940
January 6, 1941
January 6, 1942

State of the Union Address

Franklin D. Roosevelt

January 3, 1934

Mr. President, Mr. Speaker, Senators and Representatives in Congress:

I come before you at the opening of the Regular Session of the 73d Congress, not to make requests for special or detailed items of legislation; I come, rather, to counsel with you, who, like myself, have been selected to carry out a mandate of the whole people, in order that without partisanship you and I may cooperate to continue the restoration of our national wellbeing and, equally important, to build on the ruins of the past a new structure designed better to meet the present problems of modern civilization.

Such a structure includes not only the relations of industry and agriculture and finance to each other but also the effect which all of these three have on our individual citizens and on the whole people as a Nation.

Now that we are definitely in the process of recovery, lines have been rightly drawn between those to whom this recovery means a return to old methods—and the number of these people is small—and those for whom recovery means a reform of many old methods, a permanent readjustment of many of our ways of thinking and therefore of many of our social and economic arrangements. . . . .

Civilization cannot go back; civilization must not stand still. We have undertaken new methods. It is our task to perfect, to improve, to alter when necessary, but in all cases to go forward. To consolidate what we are doing, to make our economic and social structure capable of dealing with modern life is the joint task of the legislative, the judicial, and the executive branches of the national Government.

Without regard to party, the overwhelming majority of our people seek a greater opportunity for humanity to prosper and find happiness. They recognize that human welfare has not increased and does not increase through mere materialism and luxury, but that it does progress through integrity, unselfishness, responsibility and justice.

In the past few months, as a result of our action, we have demanded of many citizens that they surrender certain licenses to do as they please in their business relationships; but we have asked this in exchange for the protection which the State can give against exploitation by their fellow men or by combinations of their fellow men.

I congratulate this Congress upon the courage, the earnestness and the efficiency with which you met the crisis at the Special Session. It was your fine understanding of the national problem that furnished the example which the country has so splendidly followed. I venture to say that the task confronting the First Congress of 1789 was no greater than your own.

I shall not attempt to set forth either the many phases of the crisis which we experienced last March, or the many measures which you and I undertook during the Special Session that we might initiate recovery and reform.

It is sufficient that I should speak in broad terms of the results of our common counsel. The credit of the Government has been fortified by drastic reduction in the cost of its permanent agencies through the Economy Act.

With the twofold purpose of strengthening the whole financial structure and of arriving eventually at a medium of exchange which over the years will have less variable purchasing and debt paying power for our people than that of the past, I have used the authority granted me to purchase all American-produced gold and silver and to buy additional gold in the world markets. Careful investigation and constant study prove that in the matter of foreign exchange rates certain of our sister Nations find themselves so handicapped by internal and other conditions that they feel unable at this time to enter into stabilization discussion based on permanent and world-wide objectives.

The overwhelming majority of the banks, both national and State, which reopened last spring, are in sound condition and have been brought within the protection of Federal insurance. In the case of those banks which were not permitted to reopen, nearly six hundred million dollars of frozen deposits are being restored to the depositors through the assistance of the national Government.

We have made great strides toward the objectives of the National Industrial Recovery Act, for not only have several millions of our unemployed been restored to work, but industry is organizing itself with a greater understanding that reasonable profits can be earned while at the same time protection can be assured to guarantee to labor adequate pay and proper conditions of work. Child labor is abolished. Uniform standards of hours and wages apply today to 95 percent of industrial employment within the field of the National Industrial Recovery Act. We seek the definite end of preventing combinations in furtherance of monopoly and in restraint of trade, while at the same time we seek to prevent ruinous rivalries within industrial groups which in many cases resemble the gang wars of the underworld and in which the real victim in every case is the public itself.

Under the authority of this Congress, we have brought the component parts of each industry together around a common table, just as we have brought problems affecting labor to a common meeting ground. Though the machinery, hurriedly devised, may need readjustment from time to time, nevertheless I think you will agree with me that we have created a permanent feature of our modernized industrial structure and that it will continue under the supervision but not the arbitrary dictation of Government itself.

You recognized last spring that the most serious part of the debt burden affected those who stood in danger of losing their farms and their homes. I am glad to tell you that refinancing in both of these cases is proceeding with good success and in all probability within the financial limits set by the Congress.

But agriculture had suffered from more than its debts. Actual experience with the operation of the Agricultural Adjustment Act leads to my belief that thus far the experiment of seeking a balance between production and consumption is succeeding and has made progress entirely in line with reasonable expectations toward the restoration of farm prices to parity. I continue in my conviction that industrial progress and prosperity can only be attained by bringing the purchasing power of that portion of our population which in one form or another is dependent upon agriculture up to a level which will restore a proper balance between every section of the country and between every form of work.

In this field, through carefully planned flood control, power development and land-use policies in the Tennessee Valley and in other, great watersheds, we are seeking the elimination of waste, the removal of poor lands from agriculture and the encouragement of small local industries, thus furthering this principle of a better balanced national life. We recognize the great ultimate cost of the application of this rounded policy to every part off the Union. Today we are creating heavy obligations to start the work because of the great unemployment needs of the moment. I look forward, however, to the time in the not distant future, when annual appropriations, wholly covered by current revenue, will enable the work to proceed under a national plan. Such a national plan will, in a generation or two, return many times the money spent on it; more important, it will eliminate the use of inefficient tools, conserve and increase natural resources, prevent waste, and enable millions of our people to take better advantage of the opportunities which God has given our country.

I cannot, unfortunately, present to you a picture of complete optimism regarding world affairs.

The delegation representing the United States has worked in close cooperation with the other American Republics assembled at Montevideo to make that conference an outstanding success. We have, I hope, made it clear to our neighbors that we seek with them future avoidance of territorial expansion and of interference by one Nation in the internal affairs of another. Furthermore, all of us are seeking the restoration of commerce in ways which will preclude the building up of large favorable trade balances by any one Nation at the expense of trade debits on the part of other Nations.

In other parts of the world, however, fear of immediate or future aggression and with it the spending of vast sums on armament and the continued building up of defensive trade barriers prevent any great progress in peace or trade agreements. I have made it clear that the United States cannot take part in political arrangements in Europe but that we stand ready to cooperate at any time in practicable measures on a world basis looking to immediate reduction of armaments and the lowering of the barriers against commerce.

I expect to report to you later in regard to debts owed the Government and people of this country by the Governments and peoples of other countries. Several Nations, acknowledging the debt, have paid in small part; other Nations have failed to pay. One Nation—Finland—has paid the installments due this country in full.

Returning to home problems, we have been shocked by many notorious examples of injuries done our citizens by persons or groups who have been living off their neighbors by the use of methods either unethical or criminal.

In the first category—a field which does not involve violations of the letter of our laws—practices have been brought to light which have shocked those who believed that we were in the past generation raising the ethical standards of business. They call for stringent preventive or regulatory measures. I am speaking of those individuals who have evaded the spirit and purpose of our tax laws, of those high officials of banks or corporations who have grown rich at the expense of their stockholders or the public, of those reckless speculators with their own or other people's money whose operations have injured the values of the farmers' crops and the savings of the poor.

In the other category, crimes of organized banditry, coldblooded shooting, lynching and kidnapping have threatened our security.

These violations of ethics and these violations of law call on the strong arm of Government for their immediate suppression; they call also on the country for an aroused public opinion.

The adoption of the Twenty-first Amendment should give material aid to the elimination of those new forms of crime which came from the illegal traffic in liquor.

I shall continue to regard it as my duty to use whatever means may be necessary to supplement State, local and private agencies for the relief of suffering caused by unemployment. With respect to this question, I have recognized the dangers inherent in the direct giving of relief and have sought the means to provide not mere relief, but the opportunity for useful and remunerative work. We shall, in the process of recovery, seek to move as rapidly as possible from direct relief to publicly supported work and from that to the rapid restoration of private employment.

It is to the eternal credit of the American people that this tremendous readjustment of our national life is being accomplished peacefully, without serious dislocation, with only a minimum of injustice and with a great, willing spirit of cooperation throughout the country.

Disorder is not an American habit. Self-help and self-control are the essence of the American tradition—not of necessity the form of that tradition, but its spirit. The program itself comes from the American people.

It is an integrated program, national in scope. Viewed in the large, it is designed to save from destruction and to keep for the future the genuinely important values created by modern society. The vicious and wasteful parts of that society we could not save if we wished; they have chosen the way of self-destruction. We would save useful mechanical invention, machine production, industrial efficiency, modern means of communication, broad education. We would save and encourage the slowly growing impulse among consumers to enter the industrial market place equipped with sufficient organization to insist upon fair prices and honest sales.

But the unnecessary expansion of industrial plants, the waste of natural resources, the exploitation of the consumers of natural monopolies, the accumulation of stagnant surpluses, child labor, and the ruthless exploitation of all labor, the encouragement of speculation with other people's money, these were consumed in the fires that they themselves kindled; we must make sure that as we reconstruct our life there be no soil in which such weeds can grow again.

We have plowed the furrow and planted the good seed; the hard beginning is over. If we would reap the full harvest, we must cultivate the soil where this good seed is sprouting and the plant is reaching up to mature growth.

A final personal word. I know that each of you will appreciate that. I am speaking no mere politeness when I assure you how much I value the fine relationship that we have shared during these months of hard and incessant work. Out of these friendly contacts we are, fortunately, building a strong and permanent tie between the legislative and executive branches of the Government. The letter of the Constitution wisely declared a separation, but the impulse of common purpose declares a union. In this spirit we join once more in serving the American people.

State of the Union Address

Franklin D. Roosevelt

January 7, 1943

Mr. Vice President, Mr. Speaker, Members of the Seventy-eighth Congress:

This Seventy-eighth Congress assembles in one of the great moments in the history of the Nation. The past year was perhaps the most crucial for modern civilization; the coming year will be filled with violent conflicts— yet with high promise of better things.

We must appraise the events of 1942 according to their relative importance; we must exercise a sense of proportion.

First in importance in the American scene has been the inspiring proof of the great qualities of our fighting men. They have demonstrated these qualities in adversity as well as in victory. As long as our flag flies over this Capitol, Americans will honor the soldiers, sailors, and marines who fought our first battles of this war against overwhelming odds the heroes, living and dead, of Wake and Bataan and Guadalcanal, of the Java Sea and Midway and the North Atlantic convoys. Their unconquerable spirit will live forever.

By far the largest and most important developments in the whole world-wide strategic picture of 1942 were the events of the long fronts in Russia: first, the implacable defense of Stalingrad; and, second, the offensives by the Russian armies at various points that started in the latter part of November and which still roll on with great force and effectiveness.

The other major events of the year were: the series of Japanese advances in the Philippines, the East Indies, Malaya, and Burma; the stopping of that Japanese advance in the mid-Pacific, the South Pacific, and the Indian Oceans; the successful defense of the Near East by the British counterattack through Egypt and Libya; the American-British occupation of North Africa. Of continuing importance in the year 1942 were the unending and bitterly contested battles of the convoy routes, and the gradual passing of air superiority from the Axis to the United Nations.

The Axis powers knew that they must win the war in 1942—or eventually lose everything. I do not need to tell you that our enemies did not win the war in 1942.

In the Pacific area, our most important victory in 1942 was the air and naval battle off Midway Island. That action is historically important because it secured for our use communication lines stretching thousands of miles in every direction. In placing this emphasis on the Battle of Midway, I am not unmindful of other successful actions in the Pacific, in the air and on land and afloat— especially those on the Coral Sea and New Guinea and in the Solomon Islands. But these actions were essentially defensive. They were part of the delaying strategy that characterized this phase of the war.

During this period we inflicted steady losses upon the enemy—great losses of Japanese planes and naval vessels, transports and cargo ships. As early as one year ago, we set as a primary task in the war of the Pacific a day-by-day and week-by-week and month-by-month destruction of more Japanese war materials than Japanese industry could replace. Most certainly, that task has been and is being performed by our fighting ships and planes. And a large part of this task has been accomplished by the gallant crews of our American submarines who strike on the other side of the Pacific at Japanese ships—right up at the very mouth of the harbor of Yokohama.

We know that as each day goes by, Japanese strength in ships and planes is going down and down, and American strength in ships and planes is going up and up. And so I sometimes feel that the eventual outcome can now be put on a mathematical basis. That will become evident to the Japanese people themselves when we strike at their own home islands, and bomb them constantly from the air.

And in the attacks against Japan, we shall be joined with the heroic people of China—that great people whose ideals of peace are so closely akin to our own. Even today we are flying as much lend-lease material into China as ever traversed the Burma Road, flying it over mountains 17,000 feet high, flying blind through sleet and snow. We shall overcome all the formidable obstacles, and get the battle equipment into China to shatter the power of our common enemy. From this war, China will realize the security, the prosperity and the dignity, which Japan has sought so ruthlessly to destroy.

The period of our defensive attrition in the Pacific is drawing to a close. Now our aim is to force the Japanese to fight. Last year, we stopped them. This year, we intend to advance.

Turning now to the European theater of war, during this past year it was clear that our first task was to lessen the concentrated pressure on the Russian front by compelling Germany to divert part of her manpower and equipment to another theater of war. After months of secret planning and preparation in the utmost detail, an enormous amphibious expedition was embarked for French North Africa from the United States and the United Kingdom in literally hundreds of ships. It reached its objectives with very small losses, and has already produced an important effect upon the whole situation of the war. It has opened to attack what Mr. Churchill well described as "the under-belly of the Axis," and it has removed the always dangerous threat of an Axis attack through West Africa against the South Atlantic Ocean and the continent of South America itself.

The well-timed and splendidly executed offensive from Egypt by the British Eighth Army was a part of the same major strategy of the United Nations.

Great rains and appalling mud and very limited communications have delayed the final battles of Tunisia. The Axis is reinforcing its strong positions. But I am confident that though the fighting will be tough, when the final Allied assault is made, the last vestige of Axis power will be driven from the whole of the south shores of the Mediterranean.

Any review of the year 1942 must emphasize the magnitude and the diversity of the military activities in which this Nation has become engaged. As I speak to you, approximately one and a half million of our soldiers, sailors, marines, and fliers are in service outside of our continental limits, all through the world. Our merchant seamen, in addition, are carrying supplies to them and to our allies over every sea lane.

Few Americans realize the amazing growth of our air strength, though I am sure our enemy does. Day in and day out our forces are bombing the enemy and meeting him in combat on many different fronts in every part of the world. And for those who question the quality of our aircraft and the ability of our fliers, I point to the fact that, in Africa, we are shooting down two enemy planes to every one we lose, and in the Pacific and the Southwest Pacific we are shooting them down four to one.

We pay great tribute—the tribute of the United States of America—to the fighting men of Russia and China and Britain and the various members of the British Commonwealth—the millions of men who through the years of this war have fought our common enemies, and have denied to them the world conquest which they sought.

We pay tribute to the soldiers and fliers and seamen of others of the United Nations whose countries have been overrun by Axis hordes.

As a result of the Allied occupation of North Africa, powerful units of the French Army and Navy are going into action. They are in action with the United Nations forces. We welcome them as allies and as friends. They join with those Frenchmen who, since the dark days of June, 1940, have been fighting valiantly for the liberation of their stricken country.

We pay tribute to the fighting leaders of our allies, to Winston Churchill, to Joseph Stalin, and to the Generalissimo Chiang Kai-shek. Yes, there is a very great unanimity between the leaders of the United Nations. This unity is effective in planning and carrying out the major strategy of this war and in building up and in maintaining the lines of supplies.

I cannot prophesy. I cannot tell you when or where the United Nations are going to strike next in Europe. But we are going to strike—and strike hard. I cannot tell you whether we are going to hit them in Norway, or through the Low Countries, or in France, or through Sardinia or Sicily, or through the Balkans, or through Poland—or at several points simultaneously. But I can tell you that no matter where and when we strike by land, we and the British and the Russians will hit them from the air heavily and relentlessly. Day in and day out we shall heap tons upon tons of high explosives on their war factories and utilities and seaports.

Hitler and Mussolini will understand now the enormity of their miscalculations—that the Nazis would always have the advantage of superior air power as they did when they bombed Warsaw, and Rotterdam, and London and Coventry. That superiority has gone—forever.

Yes, the Nazis and the Fascists have asked for it—and they are going to get it.

Our forward progress in this war has depended upon our progress on the production front.

There has been criticism of the management and conduct of our war production. Much of this self-criticism has had a healthy effect. It has spurred us on. It has reflected a normal American impatience to get on with the job. We are the kind of people who are never quite satisfied with anything short of miracles.

But there has been some criticism based on guesswork and even on malicious falsification of fact. Such criticism creates doubts and creates fears, and weakens our total effort.

I do not wish to suggest that we should be completely satisfied with our production progress today, or next month, or ever. But I can report to you with genuine pride on what has been accomplished in 1942.

A year ago we set certain production goals for 1942 and for 1943. Some people, including some experts, thought that we had pulled some big figures out of a hat just to frighten the Axis. But we had confidence in the ability of our people to establish new records. And that confidence has been justified.

Of course, we realized that some production objectives would have to be changed—some of them adjusted upward, and others downward; some items would be taken out of the program altogether, and others added. This was inevitable as we gained battle experience, and as technological improvements were made.

Our 1942 airplane production and tank production fell short, numerically— stress the word numerically of the goals set a year ago. Nevertheless, we have plenty of reason to be proud of our record for 1942. We produced 48,000 military planes—more than the airplane production of Germany, Italy, and Japan put together. Last month, in December, we produced 5,500 military planes and the rate is rapidly rising. Furthermore, we must remember that as each month passes by, the averages of our types weigh more, take more man-hours to make, and have more striking power.

In tank production, we revised our schedule—and for good and sufficient reasons. As a result of hard experience in battle, we have diverted a portion of our tank-producing capacity to a stepped-up production of new, deadly field weapons, especially self-propelled artillery.

Here are some other production figures:

In 1942, we produced 56,000 combat vehicles, such as tanks and self-propelled artillery.

In 1942, we produced 670,000 machine guns, six times greater than our production in 1941 and three times greater than our total production during the year and a half of our participation in the first World War.

We produced 21,000 anti-tank guns, six times greater than our 1941 production.

We produced ten and a quarter billion rounds of small-arms ammunition, five times greater than our 1941 production and three times greater than our total production in the first World War.

We produced 181 million rounds of artillery ammunition, twelve times greater than our 1941 production and ten times greater than our total production in the first World War.

I think the arsenal of democracy is making good.

These facts and figures that I have given will give no great aid and comfort to the enemy. On the contrary, I can imagine that they will give him considerable discomfort. I suspect that Hitler and Tojo will find it difficult to explain to the German and Japanese people just why it is that "decadent, inefficient democracy" can produce such phenomenal quantities of weapons and munitions—and fighting men.

We have given the lie to certain misconceptions—which is an extremely polite word—especially the one which holds that the various blocs or groups within a free country cannot forego their political and economic differences in time of crisis and work together toward a common goal.

While we have been achieving this miracle of production, during the past year our armed forces have grown from a little over 2,000,000 to 7,000,000. In other words, we have withdrawn from the labor force and the farms some 5,000,000 of our younger workers. And in spite of this, our farmers have contributed their share to the common effort by producing the greatest quantity of food ever made available during a single year in all our history.

I wonder is there any person among us so simple as to believe that all this could have been done without creating some dislocations in our normal national life, some inconveniences, and even some hardships?

Who can have hoped to have done this without burdensome Government regulations which are a nuisance to everyone—including those who have the thankless task of administering them?

We all know that there have been mistakes—mistakes due to the inevitable process of trial and error inherent in doing big things for the first time. We all know that there have been too many complicated forms and questionnaires. I know about that. I have had to fill some of them out myself.

But we are determined to see to it that our supplies of food and other essential civilian goods are distributed on a fair and just basis—to rich and poor, management and labor, farmer and city dweller alike. We are determined to keep the cost of living at a stable level. All this has required much information. These forms and questionnaires represent an honest and sincere attempt by honest and sincere officials to obtain this information.

We have learned by the mistakes that we have made.

Our experience will enable us during the coming year to improve the necessary mechanisms of wartime economic controls, and to simplify administrative procedures. But we do not intend to leave things so lax that loopholes will be left for cheaters, for chiselers, or for the manipulators of the black market.

Of course, there have been disturbances and inconveniences—and even hardships. And there will be many, many more before we finally win. Yes, 1943 will not be an easy year for us on the home front. We shall feel in many ways in our daily lives the sharp pinch of total war.

Fortunately, there are only a few Americans who place appetite above patriotism. The overwhelming majority realize that the food we send abroad is for essential military purposes, for our own and Allied fighting forces, and for necessary help in areas that we occupy.

We Americans intend to do this great job together. In our common labors we must build and fortify the very foundation of national unity—confidence in one another.

It is often amusing, and it is sometimes politically profitable, to picture the City of Washington as a madhouse, with the Congress and the Administration disrupted with confusion and indecision and general incompetence.

However—what matters most in war is results. And the one pertinent fact is that after only a few years of preparation and only one year of warfare, we are able to engage, spiritually as well as physically, in the total waging of a total war.

Washington may be a madhouse—but only in the sense that it is the Capital City of a Nation which is fighting mad. And I think that Berlin and Rome and Tokyo, which had such contempt for the obsolete methods of democracy, would now gladly use all they could get of that same brand of madness.

And we must not forget that our achievements in production have been relatively no greater than those of the Russians and the British and the Chinese who have developed their own war industries under the incredible difficulties of battle conditions. They have had to continue work through bombings and blackouts. And they have never quit.

We Americans are in good, brave company in this war, and we are playing our own, honorable part in the vast common effort.

As spokesmen for the United States Government, you and I take off our hats to those responsible for our American production—to the owners, managers, and supervisors, to the draftsmen and the engineers, and to the workers— men and women—in factories and arsenals and shipyards and mines and mills and forests—and railroads and on highways.

We take off our hats to the farmers who have faced an unprecedented task of feeding not only a great Nation but a great part of the world.

We take off our hats to all the loyal, anonymous, untiring men and women who have worked in private employment and in Government and who have endured rationing and other stringencies with good humor and good will.

Yes, we take off our hats to all Americans who have contributed so magnificently to our common cause.

I have sought to emphasize a sense of proportion in this review of the events of the war and the needs of the war.

We should never forget the things we are fighting for. But, at this critical period of the war, we should confine ourselves to the larger objectives and not get bogged down in argument over methods and details.

We, and all the United Nations, want a decent peace and a durable peace. In the years between the end of the first World War and the beginning of the second World War, we were not living under a decent or a durable peace.

I have reason to know that our boys at the front are concerned with two broad aims beyond the winning of the war; and their thinking and their opinion coincide with what most Americans here back home are mulling over. They know, and we know, that it would be inconceivable—it would, indeed, be sacrilegious—if this Nation and the world did not attain some real, lasting good out of all these efforts and sufferings and bloodshed and death.

The men in our armed forces want a lasting peace, and, equally, they want permanent employment for themselves, their families, and their neighbors when they are mustered out at the end of the war.

Two years ago I spoke in my Annual Message of four freedoms. The blessings of two of them—freedom of speech and freedom of religion—are an essential part of the very life of this Nation; and we hope that these blessings will be granted to all men everywhere.

The people at home, and the people at the front, are wondering a little about the third freedom—freedom from want. To them it means that when they are mustered out, when war production is converted to the economy of peace, they will have the right to expect full employment—full employment for themselves and for all able-bodied men and women in America who want to work.

They expect the opportunity to work, to run their farms, their stores, to earn decent wages. They are eager to face the risks inherent in our system of free enterprise.

They do not want a postwar America which suffers from undernourishment or slums—or the dole. They want no get-rich-quick era of bogus "prosperity" which will end for them in selling apples on a street corner, as happened after the bursting of the boom in 1929.

When you talk with our young men and our young women, you will find they want to work for themselves and for their families; they consider that they have the right to work; and they know that after the last war their fathers did not gain that right.

When you talk with our young men and women, you will find that with the opportunity for employment they want assurance against the evils of all major economic hazards—assurance that will extend from the cradle to the grave. And this great Government can and must provide this assurance.

I have been told that this is no time to speak of a better America after the war. I am told it is a grave error on my part.

I dissent.

And if the security of the individual citizen, or the family, should become a subject of national debate, the country knows where I stand.

I say this now to this Seventy-eighth Congress, because it is wholly possible that freedom from want—the right of employment, the right of assurance against life's hazards—will loom very large as a task of America during the coming two years.

I trust it will not be regarded as an issue—but rather as a task for all of us to study sympathetically, to work out with a constant regard for the attainment of the objective, with fairness to all and with injustice to none.

In this war of survival we must keep before our minds not only the evil things we fight against but the good things we are fighting for. We fight to retain a great past—and we fight to gain a greater future.

Let us remember, too, that economic safety for the America of the future is threatened unless a greater economic stability comes to the rest of the world. We cannot make America an island in either a military or an economic sense. Hitlerism, like any other form of crime or disease, can grow from the evil seeds of economic as well as military feudalism.

Victory in this war is the first and greatest goal before us. Victory in the peace is the next. That means striving toward the enlargement of the security of man here and throughout the world—and, finally, striving for the fourth freedom—freedom from fear.

It is of little account for any of us to talk of essential human needs, of attaining security, if we run the risk of another World War in ten or twenty or fifty years. That is just plain common sense. Wars grow in size, in death and destruction, and in the inevitability of engulfing all Nations, in inverse ratio to the shrinking size of the world as a result of the conquest of the air. I shudder to think of what will happen to humanity, including ourselves, if this war ends in an inconclusive peace, and another war breaks out when the babies of today have grown to fighting age.

Every normal American prays that neither he nor his sons nor his grandsons will be compelled to go through this horror again.

Undoubtedly a few Americans, even now, think that this Nation can end this war comfortably and then climb back into an American hole and pull the hole in after them.

But we have learned that we can never dig a hole so deep that it would be safe against predatory animals. We have also learned that if we do not pull the fangs of the predatory animals of this world, they will multiply and grow in strength—and they will be at our throats again once more in a short generation.

Most Americans realize more clearly than ever before that modern war equipment in the hands of aggressor Nations can bring danger overnight to our own national existence or to that of any other Nation—or island—or continent.

It is clear to us that if Germany and Italy and Japan—or any one of them— remain armed at the end of this war, or are permitted to rearm, they will again, and inevitably, embark upon an ambitious career of world conquest. They must be disarmed and kept disarmed, and they must abandon the philosophy, and the teaching of that philosophy, which has brought so much suffering to the world.

After the first World War we tried to achieve a formula for permanent peace, based on a magnificent idealism. We failed. But, by our failure, we have learned that we cannot maintain peace at this stage of human development by good intentions alone.

Today the United Nations are the mightiest military coalition in all history. They represent an overwhelming majority of the population of the world. Bound together in solemn agreement that they themselves will not commit acts of aggression or conquest against any of their neighbors, the United Nations can and must remain united for the maintenance of peace by preventing any attempt to rearm in Germany, in Japan, in Italy, or in any other Nation which seeks to violate the Tenth Commandment—"Thou shalt not covet."

There are cynics, there are skeptics who say it cannot be done. The American people and all the freedom-loving peoples of this earth are now demanding that it must be done. And the will of these people shall prevail.

The very philosophy of the Axis powers is based on a profound contempt for the human race. If, in the formation of our future policy, we were guided by the same cynical contempt, then we should be surrendering to the philosophy of our enemies, and our victory would turn to defeat.

The issue of this war is the basic issue between those who believe in mankind and those who do not—the ancient issue between those who put their faith in the people and those who put their faith in dictators and tyrants. There have always been those who did not believe in the people, who attempted to block their forward movement across history, to force them back to servility and suffering and silence.

The people have now gathered their strength. They are moving forward in their might and power—and no force, no combination of forces, no trickery, deceit, or violence, can stop them now. They see before them the hope of the world—a decent, secure, peaceful life for men everywhere.

I do not prophesy when this war will end.

But I do believe that this year of 1943 will give to the United Nations a very substantial advance along the roads that lead to Berlin and Rome and Tokyo.

I tell you it is within the realm of possibility that this Seventy-eighth Congress may have the historic privilege of helping greatly to save the world from future fear.

Therefore, let us all have confidence, let us redouble our efforts.

A tremendous, costly, long-enduring task in peace as well as in war is still ahead of us.

But, as we face that continuing task, we may know that the state of this Nation is good—the heart of this Nation is sound—the spirit of this Nation is strong—the faith of this Nation is eternal.

State of the Union Address

Franklin D. Roosevelt

January 11, 1944

To the Congress:

This Nation in the past two years has become an active partner in the world's greatest war against human slavery.

We have joined with like-minded people in order to defend ourselves in a world that has been gravely threatened with gangster rule.

But I do not think that any of us Americans can be content with mere survival. Sacrifices that we and our allies are making impose upon us all a sacred obligation to see to it that out of this war we and our children will gain something better than mere survival.

We are united in determination that this war shall not be followed by another interim which leads to new disaster—that we shall not repeat the tragic errors of ostrich isolationism—that we shall not repeat the excesses of the wild twenties when this Nation went for a joy ride on a roller coaster which ended in a tragic crash.

When Mr. Hull went to Moscow in October, and when I went to Cairo and Teheran in November, we knew that we were in agreement with our allies in our common determination to fight and win this war. But there were many vital questions concerning the future peace, and they were discussed in an atmosphere of complete candor and harmony.

In the last war such discussions, such meetings, did not even begin until the shooting had stopped and the delegates began to assemble at the peace table. There had been no previous opportunities for man-to-man discussions which lead to meetings of minds. The result was a peace which was not a peace.

That was a mistake which we are not repeating in this war.

And right here I want to address a word or two to some suspicious souls who are fearful that Mr. Hull or I have made "commitments" for the future which might pledge this Nation to secret treaties, or to enacting the role of Santa Claus.

To such suspicious souls—using a polite terminology—I wish to say that Mr. Churchill, and Marshal Stalin, and Generalissimo Chiang Kai-shek are all thoroughly conversant with the provisions of our Constitution. And so is Mr. Hull. And so am I.

Of course we made some commitments. We most certainly committed ourselves to very large and very specific military plans which require the use of all Allied forces to bring about the defeat of our enemies at the earliest possible time.

But there were no secret treaties or political or financial commitments.

The one supreme objective for the future, which we discussed for each Nation individually, and for all the United Nations, can be summed up in one word: Security.

And that means not only physical security which provides safety from attacks by aggressors. It means also economic security, social security, moral security—in a family of Nations.

In the plain down-to-earth talks that I had with the Generalissimo and Marshal Stalin and Prime Minister Churchill, it was abundantly clear that they are all most deeply interested in the resumption of peaceful progress by their own peoples—progress toward a better life. All our allies want freedom to develop their lands and resources, to build up industry, to increase education and individual opportunity, and to raise standards of living.

All our allies have learned by bitter experience that real development will not be possible if they are to be diverted from their purpose by repeated wars—or even threats of war.

China and Russia are truly united with Britain and America in recognition of this essential fact:

The best interests of each Nation, large and small, demand that all freedom-loving Nations shall join together in a just and durable system of peace. In the present world situation, evidenced by the actions of Germany, Italy, and Japan, unquestioned military control over disturbers of the peace is as necessary among Nations as it is among citizens in a community. And an equally basic essential to peace is a decent standard of living for all individual men and women and children in all Nations. Freedom from fear is eternally linked with freedom from want.

There are people who burrow through our Nation like unseeing moles, and attempt to spread the suspicion that if other Nations are encouraged to raise their standards of living, our own American standard of living must of necessity be depressed.

The fact is the very contrary. It has been shown time and again that if the standard of living of any country goes up, so does its purchasing power— and that such a rise encourages a better standard of living in neighboring countries with whom it trades. That is just plain common sense—and it is the kind of plain common sense that provided the basis for our discussions at Moscow, Cairo, and Teheran.

Returning from my journeyings, I must confess to a sense of "let-down" when I found many evidences of faulty perspective here in Washington. The faulty perspective consists in overemphasizing lesser problems and thereby underemphasizing the first and greatest problem.

The overwhelming majority of our people have met the demands of this war with magnificent courage and understanding. They have accepted inconveniences; they have accepted hardships; they have accepted tragic sacrifices. And they are ready and eager to make whatever further contributions are needed to win the war as quickly as possible—if only they are given the chance to know what is required of them.

However, while the majority goes on about its great work without complaint, a noisy minority maintains an uproar of demands for special favors for special groups. There are pests who swarm through the lobbies of the

Congress and the cocktail bars of Washington, representing these special groups as opposed to the basic interests of the Nation as a whole. They have come to look upon the war primarily as a chance to make profits for themselves at the expense of their neighbors—profits in money or in terms of political or social preferment.

Such selfish agitation can be highly dangerous in wartime. It creates confusion. It damages morale. It hampers our national effort. It muddies the waters and therefore prolongs the war.

If we analyze American history impartially, we cannot escape the fact that in our past we have not always forgotten individual and selfish and partisan interests in time of war—we have not always been united in purpose and direction. We cannot overlook the serious dissensions and the lack of unity in our war of the Revolution, in our War of 1812, or in our War Between the States, when the survival of the Union itself was at stake.

In the first World War we came closer to national unity than in any previous war. But that war lasted only a year and a half, and increasing signs of disunity began to appear during the final months of the conflict.

In this war, we have been compelled to learn how interdependent upon each other are all groups and sections of the population of America.

Increased food costs, for example, will bring new demands for wage increases from all war workers, which will in turn raise all prices of all things including those things which the farmers themselves have to buy. Increased wages or prices will each in turn produce the same results. They all have a particularly disastrous result on all fixed income groups.

And I hope you will remember that all of us in this Government represent the fixed income group just as much as we represent business owners, workers, and farmers. This group of fixed income people includes: teachers, clergy, policemen, firemen, widows and minors on fixed incomes, wives and dependents of our soldiers and sailors, and old-age pensioners. They and their families add up to one-quarter of our one hundred and thirty million people. They have few or no high pressure representatives at the Capitol. In a period of gross inflation they would be the worst sufferers.

If ever there was a time to subordinate individual or group selfishness to the national good, that time is now. Disunity at home—bickerings, self-seeking partisanship, stoppages of work, inflation, business as usual, politics as usual, luxury as usual these are the influences which can undermine the morale of the brave men ready to die at the front for us here.

Those who are doing most of the complaining are not deliberately striving to sabotage the national war effort. They are laboring under the delusion that the time is past when we must make prodigious sacrifices—that the war is already won and we can begin to slacken off. But the dangerous folly of that point of view can be measured by the distance that separates our troops from their ultimate objectives in Berlin and Tokyo—and by the sum of all the perils that lie along the way.

Overconfidence and complacency are among our deadliest enemies. Last spring—after notable victories at Stalingrad and in Tunisia and against the U-boats on the high seas—overconfidence became so pronounced that war production fell off. In two months, June and July, 1943, more than a thousand airplanes that could have been made and should have been made were not made. Those who failed to make them were not on strike. They were merely saying, "The war's in the bag—so let's relax."

That attitude on the part of anyone—Government or management or labor—can lengthen this war. It can kill American boys.

Let us remember the lessons of 1918. In the summer of that year the tide turned in favor of the allies. But this Government did not relax. In fact, our national effort was stepped up. In August, 1918, the draft age limits were broadened from 21-31 to 18-45. The President called for "force to the utmost," and his call was heeded. And in November, only three months later, Germany surrendered.

That is the way to fight and win a war—all out—and not with half-an-eye on the battlefronts abroad and the other eye-and-a-half on personal, selfish, or political interests here at home.

Therefore, in order to concentrate all our energies and resources on winning the war, and to maintain a fair and stable economy at home, I recommend that the Congress adopt:

(1) A realistic tax law—which will tax all unreasonable profits, both individual and corporate, and reduce the ultimate cost of the war to our sons and daughters. The tax bill now under consideration by the Congress does not begin to meet this test.

(2) A continuation of the law for the renegotiation of war contracts—which will prevent exorbitant profits and assure fair prices to the Government. For two long years I have pleaded with the Congress to take undue profits out of war.

(3) A cost of food law—which will enable the Government (a) to place a reasonable floor under the prices the farmer may expect for his production; and (b) to place a ceiling on the prices a consumer will have to pay for the food he buys. This should apply to necessities only; and will require public funds to carry out. It will cost in appropriations about one percent of the present annual cost of the war.

(4) Early reenactment of the stabilization statute of October, 1942. This expires June 30, 1944, and if it is not extended well in advance, the country might just as well expect price chaos by summer.

We cannot have stabilization by wishful thinking. We must take positive action to maintain the integrity of the American dollar.

(5) A national service law—which, for the duration of the war, will prevent strikes, and, with certain appropriate exceptions, will make available for war production or for any other essential services every able-bodied adult in this Nation.

These five measures together form a just and equitable whole. I would not recommend a national service law unless the other laws were passed to keep down the cost of living, to share equitably the burdens of taxation, to hold the stabilization line, and to prevent undue profits.

The Federal Government already has the basic power to draft capital and property of all kinds for war purposes on a basis of just compensation.

As you know, I have for three years hesitated to recommend a national service act. Today, however, I am convinced of its necessity. Although I believe that we and our allies can win the war without such a measure, I am certain that nothing less than total mobilization of all our resources of manpower and capital will guarantee an earlier victory, and reduce the toll of suffering and sorrow and blood.

I have received a joint recommendation for this law from the heads of the War Department, the Navy Department, and the Maritime Commission. These are the men who bear responsibility for the procurement of the necessary arms and equipment, and for the successful prosecution of the war in the field. They say:

"When the very life of the Nation is in peril the responsibility for service is common to all men and women. In such a time there can be no discrimination between the men and women who are assigned by the Government to its defense at the battlefront and the men and women assigned to producing the vital materials essential to successful military operations. A prompt enactment of a National Service Law would be merely an expression of the universality of this responsibility."

I believe the country will agree that those statements are the solemn truth.

National service is the most democratic way to wage a war. Like selective service for the armed forces, it rests on the obligation of each citizen to serve his Nation to his utmost where he is best qualified.

It does not mean reduction in wages. It does not mean loss of retirement and seniority rights and benefits. It does not mean that any substantial numbers of war workers will be disturbed in their present jobs. Let these facts be wholly clear.

Experience in other democratic Nations at war—Britain, Canada, Australia, and New Zealand—has shown that the very existence of national service makes unnecessary the widespread use of compulsory power. National service has proven to be a unifying moral force based on an equal and comprehensive legal obligation of all people in a Nation at war.

There are millions of American men and women who are not in this war at all. It is not because they do not want to be in it. But they want to know where they can best do their share. National service provides that direction. It will be a means by which every man and woman can find that inner satisfaction which comes from making the fullest possible contribution to victory.

I know that all civilian war workers will be glad to be able to say many years hence to their grandchildren: "Yes, I, too, was in service in the great war. I was on duty in an airplane factory, and I helped make hundreds of fighting planes. The Government told me that in doing that I was performing my most useful work in the service of my country."

It is argued that we have passed the stage in the war where national service is necessary. But our soldiers and sailors know that this is not true. We are going forward on a long, rough road—and, in all journeys, the last miles are the hardest. And it is for that final effort—for the total defeat of our enemies—that we must mobilize our total resources. The national war program calls for the employment of more people in 1944 than in 1943.

It is my conviction that the American people will welcome this win-the-war measure which is based on the eternally just principle of "fair for one, fair for all."

It will give our people at home the assurance that they are standing four-square behind our soldiers and sailors. And it will give our enemies demoralizing assurance that we mean business—that we, 130,000,000 Americans, are on the march to Rome, Berlin, and Tokyo.

I hope that the Congress will recognize that, although this is a political year, national service is an issue which transcends politics. Great power must be used for great purposes.

As to the machinery for this measure, the Congress itself should determine its nature—but it should be wholly nonpartisan in its make-up.

Our armed forces are valiantly fulfilling their responsibilities to our country and our people. Now the Congress faces the responsibility for taking those measures which are essential to national security in this the most decisive phase of the Nation's greatest war.

Several alleged reasons have prevented the enactment of legislation which would preserve for our soldiers and sailors and marines the fundamental prerogative of citizenship—the right to vote. No amount of legalistic argument can becloud this issue in the eyes of these ten million American citizens. Surely the signers of the Constitution did not intend a document which, even in wartime, would be construed to take away the franchise of any of those who are fighting to preserve the Constitution itself.

Our soldiers and sailors and marines know that the overwhelming majority of them will be deprived of the opportunity to vote, if the voting machinery is left exclusively to the States under existing State laws—and that there is no likelihood of these laws being changed in time to enable them to vote at the next election. The Army and Navy have reported that it will be impossible effectively to administer forty-eight different soldier voting laws. It is the duty of the Congress to remove this unjustifiable discrimination against the men and women in our armed forces—and to do it as quickly as possible.

It is our duty now to begin to lay the plans and determine the strategy for the winning of a lasting peace and the establishment of an American standard of living higher than ever before known. We cannot be content, no matter how high that general standard of living may be, if some fraction of our people—whether it be one-third or one-fifth or one-tenth—is ill-fed, ill-clothed, ill housed, and insecure.

This Republic had its beginning, and grew to its present strength, under the protection of certain inalienable political rights—among them the right of free speech, free press, free worship, trial by jury, freedom from unreasonable searches and seizures. They were our rights to life and liberty.

As our Nation has grown in size and stature, however—as our industrial economy expanded—these political rights proved inadequate to assure us equality in the pursuit of happiness.

We have come to a clear realization of the fact that true individual freedom cannot exist without economic security and independence. "Necessitous men are not free men." People who are hungry and out of a job are the stuff of which dictatorships are made.

In our day these economic truths have become accepted as self-evident. We have accepted, so to speak, a second Bill of Rights under which a new basis of security and prosperity can be established for all regardless of station, race, or creed.

Among these are:

The right to a useful and remunerative job in the industries or shops or farms or mines of the Nation;

The right to earn enough to provide adequate food and clothing and recreation;

The right of every farmer to raise and sell his products at a return which will give him and his family a decent living;

The right of every businessman, large and small, to trade in an atmosphere of freedom from unfair competition and domination by monopolies at home or abroad;

The right of every family to a decent home;

The right to adequate medical care and the opportunity to achieve and enjoy good health;

The right to adequate protection from the economic fears of old age, sickness, accident, and unemployment;

The right to a good education.

All of these rights spell security. And after this war is won we must be prepared to move forward, in the implementation of these rights, to new goals of human happiness and well-being.

America's own rightful place in the world depends in large part upon how fully these and similar rights have been carried into practice for our citizens. For unless there is security here at home there cannot be lasting peace in the world.

One of the great American industrialists of our day—a man who has rendered yeoman service to his country in this crisis—recently emphasized the grave dangers of "rightist reaction" in this Nation. All clear-thinking businessmen share his concern. Indeed, if such reaction should develop—if history were to repeat itself and we were to return to the so-called "normalcy" of the 1920's—then it is certain that even though we shall have conquered our enemies on the battlefields abroad, we shall have yielded to the spirit of Fascism here at home.

I ask the Congress to explore the means for implementing this economic bill of rights—for it is definitely the responsibility of the Congress so to do. Many of these problems are already before committees of the Congress in the form of proposed legislation. I shall from time to time communicate with the Congress with respect to these and further proposals. In the event that no adequate program of progress is evolved, I am certain that the Nation will be conscious of the fact.

Our fighting men abroad—and their families at home—expect such a program and have the right to insist upon it. It is to their demands that this Government should pay heed rather than to the whining demands of selfish pressure groups who seek to feather their nests while young Americans are dying.

The foreign policy that we have been following—the policy that guided us at Moscow, Cairo, and Teheran—is based on the common sense principle which was best expressed by Benjamin Franklin on July 4, 1776: "We must all hang together, or assuredly we shall all hang separately."

I have often said that there are no two fronts for America in this war. There is only one front. There is one line of unity which extends from the hearts of the people at home to the men of our attacking forces in our farthest outposts. When we speak of our total effort, we speak of the factory and the field, and the mine as well as of the battleground—we speak of the soldier and the civilian, the citizen and his Government.

Each and every one of us has a solemn obligation under God to serve this Nation in its most critical hour—to keep this Nation great—to make this Nation greater in a better world.

State of the Union Address

Franklin D. Roosevelt

January 6, 1945

To the Congress:

In considering the State of the Union, the war and the peace that is to follow are naturally uppermost in the minds of all of us.

This war must be waged—it is being waged—with the greatest and most persistent intensity. Everything we are and have is at stake. Everything we are and have will be given. American men, fighting far from home, have already won victories which the world will never forget.

We have no question of the ultimate victory. We have no question of the cost. Our losses will be heavy.

We and our allies will go on fighting together to ultimate total victory.

We have seen a year marked, on the whole, by substantial progress toward victory, even though the year ended with a setback for our arms, when the Germans launched a ferocious counter-attack into Luxembourg and Belgium with the obvious objective of cutting our line in the center.

Our men have fought with indescribable and unforgettable gallantry under most difficult conditions, and our German enemies have sustained considerable losses while failing to obtain their objectives.

The high tide of this German effort was reached two days after Christmas. Since then we have reassumed the offensive, rescued the isolated garrison at Bastogne, and forced a German withdrawal along the whole line of the salient. The speed with which we recovered from this savage attack was largely possible because we have one supreme commander in complete control of all the Allied armies in France. General Eisenhower has faced this period of trial with admirable calm and resolution and with steadily increasing success. He has my complete confidence.

Further desperate attempts may well be made to break our lines, to slow our progress. We must never make the mistake of assuming that the Germans are beaten until the last Nazi has surrendered.

And I would express another most serious warning against the poisonous effects of enemy propaganda.

The wedge that the Germans attempted to drive in western Europe was less dangerous in actual terms of winning the war than the wedges which they are continually attempting to drive between ourselves and our allies.

Every little rumor which is intended to weaken our faith in our allies is like an actual enemy agent in our midst—seeking to sabotage our war effort. There are, here and there, evil and baseless rumors against the Russians—rumors against the British—rumors against our own American commanders in the field.

When you examine these rumors closely, you will observe that every one of them bears the same trade-mark—"Made in Germany."

We must resist this divisive propaganda—we must destroy it—with the same strength and the same determination that our fighting men are displaying as they resist and destroy the panzer divisions.

In Europe, we shall resume the attack and—despite temporary setbacks here or there—we shall continue the attack relentlessly until Germany is completely defeated.

It is appropriate at this time to review the basic strategy which has guided us through three years of war, and which will lead, eventually, to total victory.

The tremendous effort of the first years of this war was directed toward the concentration of men and supplies in the various theaters of action at the points where they could hurt our enemies most.

It was an effort—in the language of the military men—of deployment of our forces. Many battles—essential battles—were fought; many victories—vital victories—were won. But these battles and these victories were fought and won to hold back the attacking enemy, and to put us in positions from which we and our allies could deliver the final, decisive blows.

In the beginning our most important military task was to prevent our enemies—the strongest and most violently aggressive powers that ever have threatened civilization—from winning decisive victories. But even while we were conducting defensive, delaying actions, we were looking forward to the time when we could wrest the initiative from our enemies and place our superior resources of men and materials into direct competition with them.

It was plain then that the defeat of either enemy would require the massing of overwhelming forces—ground, sea, and air—in positions from which we and our allies could strike directly against the enemy homelands and destroy the Nazi and Japanese war machines.

In the case of Japan, we had to await the completion of extensive preliminary operations—operations designed to establish secure supply lines through the Japanese outer-zone defenses. This called for overwhelming sea power and air power—supported by ground forces strategically employed against isolated outpost garrisons.

Always—from the very day we were attacked—it was right militarily as well as morally to reject the arguments of those shortsighted people who would have had us throw Britain and Russia to the Nazi wolves and concentrate against the Japanese. Such people urged that we fight a purely defensive war against Japan while allowing the domination of all the rest of the world by Nazism and Fascism.

In the European theater the necessary bases for the massing of ground and air power against Germany were already available in Great Britain. In the Mediterranean area we could begin ground operations against major elements of the German Army as rapidly as we could put troops in the field, first in North Africa and then in Italy.

Therefore, our decision was made to concentrate the bulk of our ground and air forces against Germany until her utter defeat. That decision was based on all these factors; and it was also based on the realization that, of our two enemies,

Germany would be more able to digest quickly her conquests, the more able quickly to convert the manpower and resources of her conquered territory into a war potential.

We had in Europe two active and indomitable allies—Britain and the Soviet Union—and there were also the heroic resistance movements in the occupied countries, constantly engaging and harassing the Germans. We cannot forget how Britain held the line, alone, in 1940 and 1941; and at the same time, despite ferocious bombardment from the air, built up a tremendous armaments industry which enabled her to take the offensive at El Alamein in 1942.

We cannot forget the heroic defense of Moscow and Leningrad and Stalingrad, or the tremendous Russian offensives of 1943 and 1944 which destroyed formidable German armies.

Nor can we forget how, for more than seven long years, the Chinese people have been sustaining the barbarous attacks of the Japanese and containing large enemy forces on the vast areas of the Asiatic mainland.

In the future we must never forget the lesson that we have learned—that we must have friends who will work with us in peace as they have fought at our side in war.

As a result of the combined effort of the Allied forces, great military victories were achieved in 1944: The liberation of France, Belgium, Greece, and parts of The Netherlands, Norway, Poland, Yugoslavia, and Czechoslovakia; the surrender of Rumania and Bulgaria; the invasion of Germany itself and Hungary; the steady march through the Pacific islands to the Philippines, Guam, and Saipan; and the beginnings of a mighty air offensive against the Japanese islands.

Now, as this Seventy-ninth Congress meets, we have reached the most critical phase of the war.

The greatest victory of the last year was, of course, the successful breach on June 6, 1944, of the German "impregnable" seawall of Europe and the victorious sweep of the Allied forces through France and Belgium and Luxembourg—almost to the Rhine itself.

The cross-channel invasion of the Allied armies was the greatest amphibious operation in the history of the world. It overshadowed all other operations in this or any other war in its immensity. Its success is a tribute to the fighting courage of the soldiers who stormed the beaches—to the sailors and merchant seamen who put the soldiers ashore and kept them supplied—and to the military and naval leaders who achieved a real miracle of planning and execution. And it is also a tribute to the ability of two Nations, Britain and America, to plan together, and work together, and fight together in perfect cooperation and perfect harmony.

This cross-channel invasion was followed in August by a second great amphibious operation, landing troops in southern France. In this, the same cooperation and the same harmony existed between the American, French, and other Allied forces based in North Africa and Italy.

The success of the two invasions is a tribute also to the ability of many men and women to maintain silence, when a few careless words would have imperiled the lives of hundreds of thousands, and would have jeopardized the whole vast undertakings.

These two great operations were made possible by success in the Battle of the Atlantic.

Without this success over German submarines, we could not have built up our invasion forces or air forces in Great Britain, nor could we have kept a steady stream of supplies flowing to them after they had landed in France.

The Nazis, however, may succeed in improving their submarines and their crews. They have recently increased their U-boat activity. The Battle of the Atlantic—like all campaigns in this war—demands eternal vigilance. But the British, Canadian, and other Allied navies, together with our own, are constantly on the alert.

The tremendous operations in western Europe have overshadowed in the public mind the less spectacular but vitally important Italian front. Its place in the strategic conduct of the war in Europe has been obscured, and—by some people unfortunately—underrated.

It is important that any misconception on that score be corrected—now.

What the Allied forces in Italy are doing is a well-considered part in our strategy in Europe, now aimed at only one objective—the total defeat of the Germans. These valiant forces in Italy are continuing to keep a substantial portion of the German Army under constant pressure—including some 20 first-line German divisions and the necessary supply and transport and replacement troops—all of which our enemies need so badly elsewhere.

Over very difficult terrain and through adverse weather conditions, our Fifth Army and the British Eighth Army—reinforced by units from other United Nations, including a brave and well equipped unit of the Brazilian Army—have, in the past year, pushed north through bloody Cassino and the Anzio beachhead, and through Rome until now they occupy heights overlooking the valley of the Po.

The greatest tribute which can be paid to the courage and fighting ability of these splendid soldiers in Italy is to point out that although their strength is about equal to that of the Germans they oppose, the Allies have been continuously on the offensive.

That pressure, that offensive, by our troops in Italy will continue.

The American people—and every soldier now fighting in the Apennines—should remember that the Italian front has not lost any of the importance which it had in the days when it was the only Allied front in Europe.

In the Pacific during the past year, we have conducted the fastest-moving offensive in the history of modern warfare. We have driven the enemy back more than 3,000 miles across the Central Pacific. A year ago, our conquest of Tarawa was a little more than a month old.

A year ago, we were preparing for our invasion of Kwajalein, the second of our great strides across the Central Pacific to the Philippines.

A year ago, General MacArthur was still fighting in New Guinea almost 1,500 miles from his present position in the Philippine Islands.

We now have firmly established bases in the Mariana Islands, from which our Super fortresses bomb Tokyo itself—and will continue to blast Japan in ever-increasing numbers.

Japanese forces in the Philippines have been cut in two. There is still hard fighting ahead—costly fighting. But the liberation of the Philippines will mean that Japan has been largely cut off from her conquests in the East Indies.

The landing of our troops on Leyte was the largest amphibious operation thus far conducted in the Pacific.

Moreover, these landings drew the Japanese Fleet into the first great sea battle which Japan has risked in almost two years. Not since the night engagements around Guadalcanal in November-December, 1942, had our Navy been able to come to grips with major units of the Japanese Fleet. We had brushed against their fleet in the first battle of the Philippine Sea in June, 1944, but not until last October were we able really to engage a major portion of the Japanese Navy in actual combat. The naval engagement which raged for three days was the heaviest blow ever struck against Japanese sea power.

As a result of that battle, much of what is left of the Japanese Fleet has been driven behind the screen of islands that separates the Yellow Sea, the China Sea, and the Sea of Japan from the Pacific.

Our Navy looks forward to any opportunity which the lords of the Japanese Navy will give us to fight them again.

The people of this Nation have a right to be proud of the courage and fighting ability of the men in the armed forces—on all fronts. They also have a right to be proud of American leadership which has guided their sons into battle.

The history of the generalship of this war has been a history of teamwork and cooperation, of skill and daring. Let me give you one example out of last year's operations in the Pacific.

Last September Admiral Halsey led American naval task forces into Philippine waters and north to the East China Sea, and struck heavy blows at Japanese air and sea power.

At that time it was our plan to approach the Philippines by further stages, taking islands which we may call A, C, and E. However, Admiral Halsey reported that a direct attack on Leyte appeared feasible. When General MacArthur received the reports from Admiral Halsey's task forces, he also concluded that it might be possible to attack the Japanese in the Philippines directly—bypassing islands A, C, and E.

Admiral Nimitz thereupon offered to make available to General MacArthur several divisions which had been scheduled to take the intermediate objectives. These discussions, conducted at great distances, all took place in one day.

General MacArthur immediately informed the Joint Chiefs of Staff here in Washington that he was prepared to initiate plans for an attack on Leyte in October. Approval of the change in plan was given on the same day.

Thus, within the space of 24 hours, a major change of plans was accomplished which involved Army and Navy forces from two different theaters of operations—a change which hastened the liberation of the Philippines and the final day of victory—a change which saved lives which would have been expended in the capture of islands which are now neutralized far behind our lines.

Our over-all strategy has not neglected the important task of rendering all possible aid to China. Despite almost insuperable difficulties, we increased this aid during 1944. At present our aid to China must be accomplished by air transport—there is no other way. By the end of 1944, the Air Transport Command was carrying into China a tonnage of supplies three times as great as that delivered a year ago, and much more, each month, than the Burma Road ever delivered at its peak.

Despite the loss of important bases in China, the tonnage delivered by air transport has enabled General Chennault's Fourteenth Air Force, which includes many Chinese flyers, to wage an effective and aggressive campaign against the Japanese. In 1944 aircraft of the Fourteenth Air Force flew more than 35,000 sorties against the Japanese and sank enormous tonnage of enemy shipping, greatly diminishing the usefulness of the China Sea lanes.

British, Dominion, and Chinese forces together with our own have not only held the line in Burma against determined Japanese attacks but have gained bases of considerable importance to the supply line into China.

The Burma campaigns have involved incredible hardship, and have demanded exceptional fortitude and determination. The officers and men who have served with so much devotion in these far distant jungles and mountains deserve high honor from their countrymen.

In all of the far-flung operations of our own armed forces—on land, and sea and in the air—the final job, the toughest job, has been performed by the average, easy-going, hard-fighting young American, who carries the weight of battle on his own shoulders.

It is to him that we and all future generations of Americans must pay grateful tribute.

But—it is of small satisfaction to him to know that monuments will be raised to him in the future. He wants, he needs, and he is entitled to insist upon, our full and active support—now.

Although unprecedented production figures have made possible our victories, we shall have to increase our goals even more in certain items.

Peak deliveries of supplies were made to the War Department in December, 1943. Due in part to cutbacks, we have not produced as much since then. Deliveries of Army supplies were down by 15 percent by July, 1944, before the upward trend was once more resumed.

Because of increased demands from overseas, the Army Service Forces in the month of October, 1944, had to increase its estimate of required production by 10 percent. But in November, one month later, the requirements for 1945 had to be increased another 10 percent, sending the production goal well above anything we have yet attained. Our armed forces in combat have steadily increased their expenditure of medium and heavy artillery ammunition. As we continue the decisive phases of this war, the munitions that we expend will mount day by day.

In October, 1944, while some were saying the war in Europe was over, the Army was shipping more men to Europe than in any previous month of the war.

One of the most urgent immediate requirements of the armed forces is more nurses. Last April the Army requirement for nurses was set at 50,000. Actual strength in nurses was then 40,000. Since that time the Army has tried to raise the additional 10,000. Active recruiting has been carried on, but the net gain in eight months has been only 2,000. There are now 42,000 nurses in the Army.

Recent estimates have increased the total number needed to 60,000. That means that 18,000 more nurses must be obtained for the Army alone and the Navy now requires 2,000 additional nurses.

The present shortage of Army nurses is reflected in undue strain on the existing force. More than a thousand nurses are now hospitalized, and part of this is due to overwork. The shortage is also indicated by the fact that 11 Army hospital units have been sent overseas without their complement of nurses. At Army hospitals in the United States there is only 1 nurse to 26 beds, instead of the recommended 1 to 15 beds.

It is tragic that the gallant women who have volunteered for service as nurses should be so overworked. It is tragic that our wounded men should ever want for the best possible nursing care.

The inability to get the needed nurses for the Army is not due to any shortage of nurses; 280,000 registered nurses are now practicing in this country. It has been estimated by the War Manpower Commission that 27,000 additional nurses could be made available to the armed forces without interfering too seriously with the needs of the civilian population for nurses.

Since volunteering has not produced the number of nurses required, I urge that the Selective Service Act be amended to provide for the induction of nurses into the armed forces. The need is too pressing to await the outcome of further efforts at recruiting.

The care and treatment given to our wounded and sick soldiers have been the best known to medical science. Those standards must be maintained at all costs. We cannot tolerate a lowering of them by failure to provide adequate nursing for the brave men who stand desperately in need of it.

In the continuing progress of this war we have constant need for new types of weapons, for we cannot afford to fight the war of today or tomorrow with the weapons of yesterday. For example, the American Army now has developed a new tank with a gun more powerful than any yet mounted on a fast-moving vehicle. The Army will need many thousands of these new tanks in 1945.

Almost every month finds some new development in electronics which must be put into production in order to maintain our technical superiority—and in order to save lives. We have to work every day to keep ahead of the enemy in radar. On D-Day, in France, with our superior new equipment, we located and then put out of operation every warning set which the Germans had along the French coast.

If we do not keep constantly ahead of our enemies in the development of new weapons, we pay for our backwardness with the life's blood of our sons.

The only way to meet these increased needs for new weapons and more of them is for every American engaged in war work to stay on his war job—for additional American civilians, men and women, not engaged in essential work, to go out and get a war job. Workers who are released because their production is cut back should get another job where production is being increased. This is no time to quit or change to less essential jobs.

There is an old and true saying that the Lord hates a quitter. And this Nation must pay for all those who leave their essential jobs—or all those who lay down on their essential jobs for nonessential reasons. And—again—that payment must be made with the life's blood of our sons.

Many critical production programs with sharply rising needs are now seriously hampered by manpower shortages. The most important Army needs are artillery ammunition, cotton duck, bombs, tires, tanks, heavy trucks, and even B-29's. In each of these vital programs, present production is behind requirements.

Navy production of bombardment ammunition is hampered by manpower shortages; so is production for its huge rocket program. Labor shortages have also delayed its cruiser and carrier programs, and production of certain types of aircraft.

There is critical need for more repair workers and repair parts; this lack delays the return of damaged fighting ships to their places in the fleet, and prevents ships now in the fighting line from getting needed overhauling.

The pool of young men under 26 classified as I-A is almost depleted. Increased replacements for the armed forces will take men now deferred who are at work in war industry. The armed forces must have an assurance of a steady flow of young men for replacements. Meeting this paramount need will be difficult, and will also make it progressively more difficult to attain the 1945 production goals.

Last year, after much consideration, I recommended that the Congress adopt a national service act as the most efficient and democratic way of insuring full production for our war requirements. This recommendation was not adopted.

I now again call upon the Congress to enact this measure for the total mobilization of all our human resources for the prosecution of the war. I urge that this be done at the earliest possible moment.

It is not too late in the war. In fact, bitter experience has shown that in this kind of mechanized warfare where new weapons are constantly being created by our enemies and by ourselves, the closer we come to the end of the war, the more pressing becomes the need for sustained war production with which to deliver the final blow to the enemy.

There are three basic arguments for a national service law:

First, it would assure that we have the right numbers of workers in the right places at the right times.

Second, it would provide supreme proof to all our fighting men that we are giving them what they are entitled to, which is nothing less than our total effort.

And, third, it would be the final, unequivocal answer to the hopes of the Nazis and the Japanese that we may become halfhearted about this war and that they can get from us a negotiated peace.

National service legislation would make it possible to put ourselves in a position to assure certain and speedy action in meeting our manpower needs.

It would be used only to the extent absolutely required by military necessities. In fact, experience in Great Britain and in other Nations at war indicates that use of the compulsory powers of national service is necessary only in rare instances.

This proposed legislation would provide against loss of retirement and seniority rights and benefits. It would not mean reduction in wages.

In adopting such legislation, it is not necessary to discard the voluntary and cooperative processes which have prevailed up to this time. This cooperation has already produced great results. The contribution of our workers to the war effort has been beyond measure. We must build on the foundations that have already been laid and supplement the measures now in operation, in order to guarantee the production that may be necessary in the critical period that lies ahead.

At the present time we are using the inadequate tools at hand to do the best we can by such expedients as manpower ceilings, and the use of priority and other powers, to induce men and women to shift from non-essential to essential war jobs.

I am in receipt of a joint letter from the Secretary of War and the Secretary of the Navy, dated January 3, 1945, which says:

"With the experience of three years of war and after the most thorough consideration, we are convinced that it is now necessary to carry out the statement made by the Congress in the joint resolutions declaring that a state of war existed with Japan and Germany: That 'to bring the conflict to a successful conclusion, all of the resources of the country are hereby pledged by the Congress of the United States.'

"In our considered judgment, which is supported by General Marshall and Admiral King, this requires total mobilization of our manpower by the passage of a national war service law. The armed forces need this legislation to hasten the day of final victory, and to keep to a minimum the cost in lives.

"National war service, the recognition by law of the duty of every citizen to do his or her part in winning the war, will give complete assurance that the need for war equipment will be filled. In the coming year we must increase the output of many weapons and supplies on short notice. Otherwise we shall not keep our production abreast of the swiftly changing needs of war. At the same time it will be necessary to draw progressively many men now engaged in war production to serve with the armed forces, and their places in war production must be filled promptly. These developments will require the addition of hundreds of thousands to those already working in war industry. We do not believe that these needs can be met effectively under present methods.

"The record made by management and labor in war industry has been a notable testimony to the resourcefulness and power of America. The needs are so great, nevertheless, that in many instances we have been forced to recall soldiers and sailors from military duty to do work of a civilian character in war production, because of the urgency of the need for equipment and because of inability to recruit civilian labor."

Pending action by the Congress on the broader aspects of national service, I recommend that the Congress immediately enact legislation which will be effective in using the services of the 4,000,000 men now classified as IV-F in whatever capacity is best for the war effort.

In the field of foreign policy, we propose to stand together with the United Nations not for the war alone but for the victory for which the war is fought.

It is not only a common danger which unites us but a common hope. Ours is an association not of Governments but of peoples—and the peoples' hope is peace. Here, as in England; in England, as in Russia; in Russia, as in China; in France, and through the continent of Europe, and throughout the world; wherever men love freedom, the hope and purpose of the people are for peace—a peace that is durable and secure.

It will not be easy to create this peoples' peace. We delude ourselves if we believe that the surrender of the armies of our enemies will make the peace we long for. The unconditional surrender of the armies of our enemies is the first and necessary step—but the first step only.

We have seen already, in areas liberated from the Nazi and the Fascist tyranny, what problems peace will bring. And we delude ourselves if we attempt to believe wishfully that all these problems can be solved overnight.

The firm foundation can be built—and it will be built. But the continuance and assurance of a living peace must, in the long run, be the work of the people themselves.

We ourselves, like all peoples who have gone through the difficult processes of liberation and adjustment, know of our own experience how great the difficulties can be. We know that they are not difficulties peculiar to any continent or any Nation. Our own Revolutionary War left behind it, in the words of one American historian, "an eddy of lawlessness and disregard of human life." There were separatist movements of one kind or another in Vermont, Pennsylvania, Virginia, Tennessee, Kentucky, and Maine. There were insurrections, open or threatened, in Massachusetts and New Hampshire. These difficulties we worked out for ourselves as the peoples of the liberated areas of Europe, faced with complex problems of adjustment, will work out their difficulties for themselves.

Peace can be made and kept only by the united determination of free and peace-loving peoples who are willing to work together—willing to help one another—willing to respect and tolerate and try to understand one another's opinions and feelings.

The nearer we come to vanquishing our enemies the more we inevitably become conscious of differences among the victors.

We must not let those differences divide us and blind us to our more important common and continuing interests in winning the war and building the peace.

International cooperation on which enduring peace must be based is not a one-way street.

Nations like individuals do not always see alike or think alike, and international cooperation and progress are not helped by any Nation assuming that it has a monopoly of wisdom or of virtue.

In the future world the misuse of power, as implied in the term "power politics," must not be a controlling factor in international relations. That is the heart of the principles to which we have subscribed. We cannot deny that power is a factor in world politics any more than we can deny its existence as a factor in national politics. But in a democratic world, as in a democratic Nation, power must be linked with responsibility, and obliged to defend and justify itself within the framework of the general good.

Perfectionism, no less than isolationism or imperialism or power politics, may obstruct the paths to international peace. Let us not forget that the retreat to isolationism a quarter of a century ago was started not by a direct attack against international cooperation but against the alleged imperfections of the peace.

In our disillusionment after the last war we preferred international anarchy to international cooperation with Nations which did not see and think exactly as we did. We gave up the hope of gradually achieving a better peace because we had not the courage to fulfill our responsibilities in an admittedly imperfect world.

We must not let that happen again, or we shall follow the same tragic road again—the road to a third world war.

We can fulfill our responsibilities for maintaining the security of our own country only by exercising our power and our influence to achieve the principles in which we believe and for which we have fought.

In August, 1941, Prime Minister Churchill and I agreed to the principles of the Atlantic Charter, these being later incorporated into the Declaration by United Nations of January 1, 1942. At that time certain isolationists protested vigorously against our right to proclaim the principles—and against the very principles themselves. Today, many of the same people are protesting against the possibility of violation of the same principles.

It is true that the statement of principles in the Atlantic Charter does not provide rules of easy application to each and every one of this war-torn world's tangled situations. But it is a good and a useful thing— it is an essential thing— to have principles toward which we can aim.

And we shall not hesitate to use our influence—and to use it now—to secure so far as is humanly possible the fulfillment of the principles of the Atlantic Charter. We have not shrunk from the military responsibilities brought on by this war. We cannot and will not shrink from the political responsibilities which follow in the wake of battle.

I do not wish to give the impression that all mistakes can be avoided and that many disappointments are not inevitable in the making of peace. But we must not this time lose the hope of establishing an international order which will be capable of maintaining peace and realizing through the years more perfect justice between Nations.

To do this we must be on our guard not to exploit and exaggerate the differences between us and our allies, particularly with reference to the peoples who have been liberated from Fascist tyranny. That is not the way to secure a better settlement of those differences or to secure international machinery which can rectify mistakes which may be made.

I should not be frank if I did not admit concern about many situations—the Greek and Polish for example. But those situations are not as easy or as simple to deal with as some spokesmen, whose sincerity I do not question, would have us believe. We have obligations, not necessarily legal, to the exiled Governments, to the underground leaders, and to our major allies who came much nearer the shadows than we did.

We and our allies have declared that it is our purpose to respect the right of all peoples to choose the form of government under which they will live and to see sovereign rights and self-government restored to those who have been forcibly deprived of them. But with internal dissension, with many citizens of liberated countries still prisoners of war or forced to labor in Germany, it is difficult to guess the kind of self-government the people really want.

During the interim period, until conditions permit a genuine expression of the people's will, we and our allies have a duty, which we cannot ignore, to use our influence to the end that no temporary or provisional authorities in the liberated countries block the eventual exercise of the peoples' right freely to choose the government and institutions under which, as freemen, they are to live.

It is only too easy for all of us to rationalize what we want to believe, and to consider those leaders we like responsible and those we dislike irresponsible. And our task is not helped by stubborn partisanship, however understandable on the part of opposed internal factions.

It is our purpose to help the peace-loving peoples of Europe to live together as good neighbors, to recognize their common interests and not to nurse their traditional grievances against one another.

But we must not permit the many specific and immediate problems of adjustment connected with the liberation of Europe to delay the establishment of permanent machinery for the maintenance of peace. Under the threat of a common danger, the United Nations joined together in war to preserve their independence and their freedom. They must now join together to make secure the independence and freedom of all peace-loving states, so that never again shall tyranny be able to divide and conquer.

International peace and well-being, like national peace and well-being, require constant alertness, continuing cooperation, and organized effort.

International peace and well-being, like national peace and well-being, can be secured only through institutions capable of life and growth.

Many of the problems of the peace are upon us even now while the conclusion of the war is still before us. The atmosphere of friendship and mutual understanding and determination to find a common ground of common understanding, which surrounded the conversations at Dumbarton Oaks, gives us reason to hope that future discussions will succeed in developing the democratic and fully integrated world security system toward which these preparatory conversations were directed.

We and the other United Nations are going forward, with vigor and resolution, in our efforts to create such a system by providing for it strong and flexible institutions of joint and cooperative action.

The aroused conscience of humanity will not permit failure in this supreme endeavor.

We believe that the extraordinary advances in the means of intercommunication between peoples over the past generation offer a practical method of advancing the mutual understanding upon which peace and the institutions of peace must rest, and it is our policy and purpose to use these great technological achievements for the common advantage of the world.

We support the greatest possible freedom of trade and commerce.

We Americans have always believed in freedom of opportunity, and equality of opportunity remains one of the principal objectives of our national life. What we believe in for individuals, we believe in also for Nations. We are opposed to restrictions, whether by public act or private arrangement, which distort and impair commerce, transit, and trade.

We have house-cleaning of our own to do in this regard. But it is our hope, not only in the interest of our own prosperity but in the interest of the prosperity of the world, that trade and commerce and access to materials and markets may be freer after this war than ever before in the history of the world.

One of the most heartening events of the year in the international field has been the renaissance of the French people and the return of the French Nation to the ranks of the United Nations. Far from having been crushed by the terror of Nazi domination, the French people have emerged with stronger faith than ever in the destiny of their country and in the soundness of the democratic ideals to which the French Nation has traditionally contributed so greatly.

During her liberation, France has given proof of her unceasing determination to fight the Germans, continuing the heroic efforts of the resistance groups under the occupation and of all those Frenchmen throughout the world who refused to surrender after the disaster of 1940.

Today, French armies are again on the German frontier, and are again fighting shoulder to shoulder with our sons.

Since our landings in Africa, we have placed in French hands all the arms and material of war which our resources and the military situation permitted.

And I am glad to say that we are now about to equip large new French forces with the most modern weapons for combat duty.

In addition to the contribution which France can make to our common victory, her liberation likewise means that her great influence will again be available in meeting the problems of peace.

We fully recognize France's vital interest in a lasting solution of the German problem and the contribution which she can make in achieving international security. Her formal adherence to the declaration by United Nations a few days ago and the proposal at the Dumbarton Oaks discussions, whereby France would receive one of the five permanent seats in the proposed Security Council, demonstrate the extent to which France has resumed her proper position of strength and leadership.

I am clear in my own mind that, as an essential factor in the maintenance of peace in the future, we must have universal military training after this war, and I shall send a special message to the Congress on this subject.

An enduring peace cannot be achieved without a strong America—strong in the social and economic sense as well as in the military sense.

In the State of the Union message last year I set forth what I considered to be an American economic bill of rights.

I said then, and I say now, that these economic truths represent a second bill of rights under which a new basis of security and prosperity can be established for all—regardless of station, race, or creed.

Of these rights the most fundamental, and one on which the fulfillment of the others in large degree depends, is the "right to a useful and remunerative job in the industries or shops or farms or mines of the Nation." In turn, others of the economic rights of American citizenship, such as the right to a decent home, to a good education, to good medical care, to social security, to reasonable farm income, will, if fulfilled, make major contributions to achieving adequate levels of employment.

The Federal Government must see to it that these rights become realities— with the help of States, municipalities, business, labor, and agriculture.

We have had full employment during the war. We have had it because the Government has been ready to buy all the materials of war which the country could produce—and this has amounted to approximately half our present productive capacity.

After the war we must maintain full employment with Government performing its peacetime functions. This means that we must achieve a level of demand and purchasing power by private consumers—farmers, businessmen, workers, professional men, housewives—which is sufficiently high to replace wartime Government demands; and it means also that we must greatly increase our export trade above the prewar level.

Our policy is, of course, to rely as much as possible on private enterprise to provide jobs. But the American people will not accept mass unemployment or mere makeshift work. There will be need for the work of everyone willing and able to work—and that means close to 60,000,000 jobs.

Full employment means not only jobs—but productive jobs. Americans do not regard jobs that pay substandard wages as productive jobs.

We must make sure that private enterprise works as it is supposed to work— on the basis of initiative and vigorous competition, without the stifling presence of monopolies and cartels.

During the war we have guaranteed investment in enterprise essential to the war effort. We should also take appropriate measures in peacetime to secure opportunities for new small enterprises and for productive business expansion for which finance would otherwise be unavailable.

This necessary expansion of our peacetime productive capacity will require new facilities, new plants, and new equipment.

It will require large outlays of money which should be raised through normal investment channels. But while private capital should finance this expansion program, the Government should recognize its responsibility for sharing part of any special or abnormal risk of loss attached to such financing.

Our full-employment program requires the extensive development of our natural resources and other useful public works. The undeveloped resources of this continent are still vast. Our river-watershed projects will add new and fertile territories to the United States. The Tennessee Valley Authority, which was constructed at a cost of $750,000,000—the cost of waging this war for less than 4 days—was a bargain. We have similar opportunities in our other great river basins. By harnessing the resources of these river basins, as we have in the Tennessee Valley, we shall provide the same kind of stimulus to enterprise as was provided by the Louisiana Purchase and the new discoveries in the West during the nineteenth century.

If we are to avail ourselves fully of the benefits of civil aviation, and if we are to use the automobiles we can produce, it will be necessary to construct thousands of airports and to overhaul our entire national highway system.

The provision of a decent home for every family is a national necessity, if this country is to be worthy of its greatness—and that task will itself create great employment opportunities. Most of our cities need extensive rebuilding. Much of our farm plant is in a state of disrepair. To make a frontal attack on the problems of housing and urban reconstruction will require thoroughgoing cooperation between industry and labor, and the Federal, State, and local Governments.

An expanded social security program, and adequate health and education programs, must play essential roles in a program designed to support individual productivity and mass purchasing power. I shall communicate further with the Congress on these subjects at a later date.

The millions of productive jobs that a program of this nature could bring are jobs in private enterprise. They are jobs based on the expanded demand for the output of our economy for consumption and investment. Through a program of this character we can maintain a national income high enough to provide for an orderly retirement of the public debt along with reasonable tax reduction.

Our present tax system geared primarily to war requirements must be revised for peacetime so as to encourage private demand.

While no general revision of the tax structure can be made until the war ends on all fronts, the Congress should be prepared to provide tax modifications at the end of the war in Europe, designed to encourage capital to invest in new enterprises and to provide jobs. As an integral part of this program to maintain high employment, we must, after the war is over, reduce or eliminate taxes which bear too heavily on consumption.

The war will leave deep disturbances in the world economy, in our national economy, in many communities, in many families, and in many individuals. It will require determined effort and responsible action of all of us to find our way back to peacetime, and to help others to find their way back to peacetime—a peacetime that holds the values of the past and the promise of the future.

If we attack our problems with determination we shall succeed. And we must succeed. For freedom and peace cannot exist without security.

During the past year the American people, in a national election, reasserted their democratic faith.

In the course of that campaign various references were made to "strife" between this Administration and the Congress, with the implication, if not the direct assertion, that this Administration and the Congress could never work together harmoniously in the service of the Nation.

It cannot be denied that there have been disagreements between the legislative and executive branches—as there have been disagreements during the past century and a half.

I think we all realize too that there are some people in this Capital City whose task is in large part to stir up dissension, and to magnify normal healthy disagreements so that they appear to be irreconcilable conflicts.

But—I think that the over-all record in this respect is eloquent: The Government of the United States of America—all branches of it—has a good record of achievement in this war.

The Congress, the Executive, and the Judiciary have worked together for the common good.

I myself want to tell you, the Members of the Senate and of the House of Representatives, how happy I am in our relationships and friendships. I have not yet had the pleasure of meeting some of the new Members in each House, but I hope that opportunity will offer itself in the near future.

We have a great many problems ahead of us and we must approach them with realism and courage.

This new year of 1945 can be the greatest year of achievement in human history.

Nineteen forty-five can see the final ending of the Nazi-Fascist reign of terror in Europe.

Nineteen forty-five can see the closing in of the forces of retribution about the center of the malignant power of imperialistic Japan.

Most important of all—1945 can and must see the substantial beginning of the organization of world peace. This organization must be the fulfillment of the promise for which men have fought and died in this war. It must be the justification of all the sacrifices that have been made—of all the dreadful misery that this world has endured.

We Americans of today, together with our allies, are making history—and I hope it will be better history than ever has been made before.

We pray that we may be worthy of the unlimited opportunities that God has given us.

State of the Union Address

Franklin D. Roosevelt

January 4, 1935

Mr. President, Mr. Speaker, Members of the Senate and of the House of Representatives:

The Constitution wisely provides that the Chief Executive shall report to the Congress on the state of the Union, for through you, the chosen legislative representatives, our citizens everywhere may fairly judge the progress of our governing. I am confident that today, in the light of the events of the past two years, you do not consider it merely a trite phrase when I tell you that I am truly glad to greet you and that I look forward to common counsel, to useful cooperation, and to genuine friendships between us.

We have undertaken a new order of things; yet we progress to it under the framework and in the spirit and intent of the American Constitution. We have proceeded throughout the Nation a measurable distance on the road toward this new order. Materially, I can report to you substantial benefits to our agricultural population, increased industrial activity, and profits to our merchants. Of equal moment, there is evident a restoration of that spirit of confidence and faith which marks the American character. Let him, who, for speculative profit or partisan purpose, without just warrant would seek to disturb or dispel this assurance, take heed before he assumes responsibility for any act which slows our onward steps.

Throughout the world, change is the order of the day. In every Nation economic problems, long in the making, have brought crises of many kinds for which the masters of old practice and theory were unprepared. In most Nations social justice, no longer a distant ideal, has become a definite goal, and ancient Governments are beginning to heed the call.

Thus, the American people do not stand alone in the world in their desire for change. We seek it through tested liberal traditions, through processes which retain all of the deep essentials of that republican form of representative government first given to a troubled world by the United States.

As the various parts in the program begun in the Extraordinary Session of the 73rd Congress shape themselves in practical administration, the unity of our program reveals itself to the Nation. The outlines of the new economic order, rising from the disintegration of the old, are apparent. We test what we have done as our measures take root in the living texture of life. We see where we have built wisely and where we can do still better.

The attempt to make a distinction between recovery and reform is a narrowly conceived effort to substitute the appearance of reality for reality itself. When a man is convalescing from illness, wisdom dictates not only cure of the symptoms, but also removal of their cause.

It is important to recognize that while we seek to outlaw specific abuses, the American objective of today has an infinitely deeper, finer and more lasting purpose than mere repression. Thinking people in almost every country of the world have come to realize certain fundamental difficulties with which civilization must reckon. Rapid changes—the machine age, the advent of universal and rapid communication and many other new factors—have brought new problems. Succeeding generations have attempted to keep pace by reforming in piecemeal fashion this or that attendant abuse. As a result, evils overlap and reform becomes confused and frustrated. We lose sight, from time to time, of our ultimate human objectives.

Let us, for a moment, strip from our simple purpose the confusion that results from a multiplicity of detail and from millions of written and spoken words.

We find our population suffering from old inequalities, little changed by vast sporadic remedies. In spite of our efforts and in spite of our talk, we have not weeded out the over privileged and we have not effectively lifted up the underprivileged. Both of these manifestations of injustice have retarded happiness. No wise man has any intention of destroying what is known as the profit motive; because by the profit motive we mean the right by work to earn a decent livelihood for ourselves and for our families.

We have, however, a clear mandate from the people, that Americans must forswear that conception of the acquisition of wealth which, through excessive profits, creates undue private power over private affairs and, to our misfortune, over public affairs as well. In building toward this end we do not destroy ambition, nor do we seek to divide our wealth into equal shares on stated occasions. We continue to recognize the greater ability of some to earn more than others. But we do assert that the ambition of the individual to obtain for him and his a proper security, a reasonable leisure, and a decent living throughout life, is an ambition to be preferred to the appetite for great wealth and great power.

I recall to your attention my message to the Congress last June in which I said: "among our objectives I place the security of the men, women and children of the Nation first." That remains our first and continuing task; and in a very real sense every major legislative enactment of this Congress should be a component part of it.

In defining immediate factors which enter into our quest, I have spoken to the Congress and the people of three great divisions:

1. The security of a livelihood through the better use of the national resources of the land in which we live.

2. The security against the major hazards and vicissitudes of life.

3. The security of decent homes.

I am now ready to submit to the Congress a broad program designed ultimately to establish all three of these factors of security—a program which because of many lost years will take many future years to fulfill.

A study of our national resources, more comprehensive than any previously made, shows the vast amount of necessary and practicable work which needs to be done for the development and preservation of our natural wealth for the enjoyment and advantage of our people in generations to come. The sound use of land and water is far more comprehensive than the mere planting of trees, building of dams, distributing of electricity or retirement of sub-marginal land. It recognizes that stranded populations, either in the country or the city, cannot have security under the conditions that now surround them.

To this end we are ready to begin to meet this problem—the intelligent care of population throughout our Nation, in accordance with an intelligent distribution of the means of livelihood for that population. A definite program for putting people to work, of which I shall speak in a moment, is a component part of this greater program of security of livelihood through the better use of our national resources.

Closely related to the broad problem of livelihood is that of security against the major hazards of life. Here also, a comprehensive survey of what has been attempted or accomplished in many Nations and in many States proves to me that the time has come for action by the national Government. I shall send to you, in a few days, definite recommendations based on these studies. These recommendations will cover the broad subjects of unemployment insurance and old age insurance, of benefits for children, form others, for the handicapped, for maternity care and for other aspects of dependency and illness where a beginning can now be made.

The third factor—better homes for our people—has also been the subject of experimentation and study. Here, too, the first practical steps can be made through the proposals which I shall suggest in relation to giving work to the unemployed.

Whatever we plan and whatever we do should be in the light of these three clear objectives of security. We cannot afford to lose valuable time in haphazard public policies which cannot find a place in the broad outlines of these major purposes. In that spirit I come to an immediate issue made for us by hard and inescapable circumstance—the task of putting people to work. In the spring of 1933 the issue of destitution seemed to stand apart; today, in the light of our experience and our new national policy, we find we can put people to work in ways which conform to, initiate and carry forward the broad principles of that policy.

The first objectives of emergency legislation of 1933 were to relieve destitution, to make it possible for industry to operate in a more rational and orderly fashion, and to put behind industrial recovery the impulse of large expenditures in Government undertakings. The purpose of the National Industrial Recovery Act to provide work for more people succeeded in a substantial manner within the first few months of its life, and the Act has continued to maintain employment gains and greatly improved working conditions in industry.

The program of public works provided for in the Recovery Act launched the Federal Government into a task for which there was little time to make preparation and little American experience to follow. Great employment has been given and is being given by these works.

More than two billions of dollars have also been expended in direct relief to the destitute. Local agencies of necessity determined the recipients of this form of relief. With inevitable exceptions the funds were spent by them with reasonable efficiency and as a result actual want of food and clothing in the great majority of cases has been overcome.

But the stark fact before us is that great numbers still remain unemployed.

A large proportion of these unemployed and their dependents have been forced on the relief rolls. The burden on the Federal Government has grown with great rapidity. We have here a human as well as an economic problem. When humane considerations are concerned, Americans give them precedence. The lessons of history, confirmed by the evidence immediately before me, show conclusively that continued dependence upon relief induces a spiritual and moral disintegration fundamentally destructive to the national fibre. To dole out relief in this way is to administer a narcotic, a subtle destroyer of the human spirit. It is inimical to the dictates of sound policy. It is in violation of the traditions of America. Work must be found for able-bodied but destitute workers.

The Federal Government must and shall quit this business of relief.

I am not willing that the vitality of our people be further sapped by the giving of cash, of market baskets, of a few hours of weekly work cutting grass, raking leaves or picking up .papers in the public parks. We must preserve not only the bodies of the unemployed from destitution but also their self-respect, their self-reliance and courage and determination. This decision brings me to the problem of what the Government should do with approximately five million unemployed now on the relief rolls.

About one million and a half of these belong to the group which in the past was dependent upon local welfare efforts. Most of them are unable for one reason or another to maintain themselves independently—for the most part, through no fault of their own. Such people, in the days before the great depression, were cared for by local efforts—by States, by counties, by towns, by cities, by churches and by private welfare agencies. It is my thought that in the future they must be cared for as they were before. I stand ready through my own personal efforts, and through the public influence of the office that I hold, to help these local agencies to get the means necessary to assume this burden.

The security legislation which I shall propose to the Congress will, I am confident, be of assistance to local effort in the care of this type of cases. Local responsibility can and will be resumed, for, after all, common sense tells us that the wealth necessary for this task existed and still exists in the local community, and the dictates of sound administration require that this responsibility be in the first instance a local one. There are, however, an additional three and one half million employable people who are on relief. With them the problem is different and the responsibility is different. This group was the victim of a nation-wide depression caused by conditions which were not local but national. The Federal Government is the only governmental agency with sufficient power and credit to meet this situation. We have assumed this task and we shall not shrink from it in the future. It is a duty dictated by every intelligent consideration of national policy to ask you to make it possible for the United States to give employment to all of these three and one half million employable people now on relief, pending their absorption in a rising tide of private employment.

It is my thought that with the exception of certain of the normal public building operations of the Government, all emergency public works shall be united in a single new and greatly enlarged plan.

With the establishment of this new system we can supersede the Federal Emergency Relief Administration with a coordinated authority which will be charged with the orderly liquidation of our present relief activities and the substitution of a national chart for the giving of work.

This new program of emergency public employment should be governed by a number of practical principles.

(1) All work undertaken should be useful—not just for a day, or a year, but useful in the sense that it affords permanent improvement in living conditions or that it creates future new wealth for the Nation.

(2) Compensation on emergency public projects should be in the form of security payments which should be larger than the amount now received as a relief dole, but at the same time not so large as to encourage the rejection of opportunities for private employment or the leaving of private employment to engage in Government work.

(3) Projects should be undertaken on which a large percentage of direct labor can be used.

(4) Preference should be given to those projects which will be self-liquidating in the sense that there is a reasonable expectation that the Government will get its money back at some future time.

(5) The projects undertaken should be selected and planned so as to compete as little as possible with private enterprises. This suggests that if it were not for the necessity of giving useful work to the unemployed now on relief, these projects in most instances would not now be undertaken.

(6) The planning of projects would seek to assure work during the coming fiscal year to the individuals now on relief, or until such time as private employment is available. In order to make adjustment to increasing private employment, work should be planned with a view to tapering it off in proportion to the speed with which the emergency workers are offered positions with private employers.

(7) Effort should be made to locate projects where they will serve the greatest unemployment needs as shown by present relief rolls, and the broad program of the National Resources Board should be freely used for guidance in selection. Our ultimate objective being the enrichment of human lives, the Government has the primary duty to use its emergency expenditures as much as possible to serve those who cannot secure the advantages of private capital.

Ever since the adjournment of the 73d Congress, the Administration has been studying from every angle the possibility and the practicability of new forms of employment. As a result of these studies I have arrived at certain very definite convictions as to the amount of money that will be necessary for the sort of public projects that I have described. I shall submit these figures in my budget message. I assure you now they will be within the sound credit of the Government.

The work itself will cover a wide field including clearance of slums, which for adequate reasons cannot be undertaken by private capital; in rural housing of several kinds, where, again, private capital is unable to function; in rural electrification; in the reforestation of the great watersheds of the Nation; in an intensified program to prevent soil erosion and to reclaim blighted areas; in improving existing road systems and in constructing national highways designed to handle modern traffic; in the elimination of grade crossings; in the extension and enlargement of the successful work of the Civilian Conservation Corps; in non-Federal works, mostly self-liquidating and highly useful to local divisions of Government; and on many other projects which the Nation needs and cannot afford to neglect.

This is the method which I propose to you in order that we may better meet this present-day problem of unemployment. Its greatest advantage is that it fits logically and usefully into the long-range permanent policy of providing the three types of security which constitute as a whole an American plan for the betterment of the future of the American people.

I shall consult with you from time to time concerning other measures of national importance. Among the subjects that lie immediately before us are the consolidation of Federal regulatory administration over all forms of transportation, the renewal and clarification of the general purposes of the National Industrial Recovery Act, the strengthening of our facilities for the prevention, detection and treatment of crime and criminals, the restoration of sound conditions in the public utilities field through abolition of the evil features of holding companies, the gradual tapering off of the emergency credit activities of Government, and improvement in our taxation forms and methods.

We have already begun to feel the bracing effect upon our economic system of a restored agriculture. The hundreds of millions of additional income that farmers are receiving are finding their way into the channels of trade. The farmers' share of the national income is slowly rising. The economic facts justify the widespread opinion of those engaged in agriculture that our provisions for maintaining a balanced production give at this time the most adequate remedy for an old and vexing problem. For the present, and especially in view of abnormal world conditions, agricultural adjustment with certain necessary improvements in methods should continue.

It seems appropriate to call attention at this time to the fine spirit shown during the past year by our public servants. I cannot praise too highly the cheerful work of the Civil Service employees, and of those temporarily working for the Government. As for those thousands in our various public agencies spread throughout the country who, without compensation, agreed to take over heavy responsibilities in connection with our various loan agencies and particularly in direct relief work, I cannot say too much. I do not think any country could show a higher average of cheerful and even enthusiastic team-work than has been shown by these men and women.

I cannot with candor tell you that general international relationships outside the borders of the United States are improved. On the surface of things many old jealousies are resurrected, old passions aroused; new strivings for armament and power, in more than one land, rear their ugly heads. I hope that calm counsel and constructive leadership will provide the steadying influence and the time necessary for the coming of new and more practical forms of representative government throughout the world wherein privilege and power will occupy a lesser place and world welfare a greater.

I believe, however, that our own peaceful and neighborly attitude toward other Nations is coming to be understood and appreciated. The maintenance of international peace is a matter in which we are deeply and unselfishly concerned. Evidence of our persistent and undeniable desire to prevent armed conflict has recently been more than once afforded.

There is no ground for apprehension that our relations with any Nation will be otherwise than peaceful. Nor is there ground for doubt that the people of most Nations seek relief from the threat and burden attaching to the false theory that extravagant armament cannot be reduced and limited by international accord.

The ledger of the past year shows many more gains than losses. Let us not forget that, in addition to saving millions from utter destitution, child labor has been for the moment outlawed, thousands of homes saved to their owners and most important of all, the morale of the Nation has been restored. Viewing the year 1934 as a whole, you and I can agree that we have a generous measure of reasons for giving thanks.

It is not empty optimism that moves me to a strong hope in the coming year. We can, if we will, make 1935 a genuine period of good feeling, sustained by a sense of purposeful progress. Beyond the material recovery, I sense a spiritual recovery as well. The people of America are turning as never before to those permanent values that are not limited to the physical objectives of life. There are growing signs of this on every hand. In the face of these spiritual impulses we are sensible of the Divine Providence to which Nations turn now, as always, for guidance and fostering care.

State of the Union Address

Franklin D. Roosevelt

January 3, 1936

Mr. President, Mr. Speaker, Members of the Senate and of the House of Representatives:

We are about to enter upon another year of the responsibility which the electorate of the United States has placed in our hands. Having come so far, it is fitting that we should pause to survey the ground which we have covered and the path which lies ahead.

On the fourth day of March, 1933, on the occasion of taking the oath of office as President of the United States, I addressed the people of our country. Need I recall either the scene or the national circumstances attending the occasion? The crisis of that moment was almost exclusively a national one. In recognition of that fact, so obvious to the millions in the streets and in the homes of America, I devoted by far the greater part of that address to what I called, and the Nation called, critical days within our own borders.

You will remember that on that fourth of March, 1933, the world picture was an image of substantial peace. International consultation and widespread hope for the bettering of relations between the Nations gave to all of us a reasonable expectation that the barriers to mutual confidence, to increased trade, and to the peaceful settlement of disputes could be progressively removed. In fact, my only reference to the field of world policy in that address was in these words: "I would dedicate this Nation to the policy of the good neighbor—the neighbor who resolutely respects himself and, because he does so, respects the rights of others—a neighbor who respects his obligations and respects the sanctity of his agreements in and with a world of neighbors."

In the years that have followed, that sentiment has remained the dedication of this Nation. Among the Nations of the great Western Hemisphere the policy of the good neighbor has happily prevailed. At no time in the four and a half centuries of modern civilization in the Americas has there existed—in any year, in any decade, in any generation in all that time—a greater spirit of mutual understanding, of common helpfulness, and of devotion to the ideals of serf-government than exists today in the twenty-one American Republics and their neighbor, the Dominion of Canada. This policy of the good neighbor among the Americas is no longer a hope, no longer an objective remaining to be accomplished. It is a fact, active, present, pertinent and effective. In this achievement, every American Nation takes an understanding part. There is neither war, nor rumor of war, nor desire for war. The inhabitants of this vast area, two hundred and fifty million strong, spreading more than eight thousand miles from the Arctic to the Antarctic, believe in, and propose to follow, the policy of the good neighbor. They wish with all their heart that the rest of the world might do likewise.

The rest of the world—Ah! there is the rub.

Were I today to deliver an Inaugural Address to the people of the United States, I could not limit my comments on world affairs to one paragraph. With much regret I should be compelled to devote the greater part to world affairs. Since the summer of that same year of 1933, the temper and the purposes of the rulers of many of the great populations in Europe and in Asia have not pointed the way either to peace or to good-will among men. Not only have peace and good-will among men grown more remote in those areas of the earth during this period, but a point has been reached where the people of the Americas must take cognizance of growing ill-will, of marked trends toward aggression, of increasing armaments, of shortening tempers—a situation which has in it many of the elements that lead to the tragedy of general war.

On those other continents many Nations, principally the smaller peoples, if left to themselves, would be content with their boundaries and willing to solve within themselves and in cooperation with their neighbors their individual problems, both economic and social. The rulers of those Nations, deep in their hearts, follow these peaceful and reasonable aspirations of their peoples. These rulers must remain ever vigilant against the possibility today or tomorrow of invasion or attack by the rulers of other peoples who fail to subscribe to the principles of bettering the human race by peaceful means.

Within those other Nations—those which today must bear the primary, definite responsibility for jeopardizing world peace—what hope lies? To say the least, there are grounds for pessimism. It is idle for us or for others to preach that the masses of the people who constitute those Nations which are dominated by the twin spirits of autocracy and aggression, are out of sympathy with their rulers, that they are allowed no opportunity to express themselves, that they would change things if they could.

That, unfortunately, is not so clear. It might be true that the masses of the people in those Nations would change the policies of their Governments if they could be allowed full freedom and full access to the processes of democratic government as we understand them. But they do not have that access; lacking it they follow blindly and fervently the lead of those who seek autocratic power.

Nations seeking expansion, seeking the rectification of injustices springing from former wars, or seeking outlets for trade, for population or even for their own peaceful contributions to the progress of civilization, fail to demonstrate that patience necessary to attain reasonable and legitimate objectives by peaceful negotiation or by an appeal to the finer instincts of world justice.

They have therefore impatiently reverted to the old belief in the law of the sword, or to the fantastic conception that they, and they alone, are chosen to fulfill a mission and that all the others among the billion and a half of human beings in the world must and shall learn from and be subject to them.

I recognize and you will recognize that these words which I have chosen with deliberation will not prove popular in any Nation that chooses to fit this shoe to its foot. Such sentiments, however, will find sympathy and understanding in those Nations where the people themselves are honestly desirous of peace but must constantly align themselves on one side or the other in the kaleidoscopic jockeying for position which is characteristic of European and Asiatic relations today. For the peace-loving Nations, and there are many of them, find that their very identity depends on their moving and moving again on the chess board of international politics.

I suggested in the spring of 1933 that 85 or 90 percent of all the people in the world were content with the territorial limits of their respective Nations and were willing further to reduce their armed forces if every other Nation in the world would agree to do likewise.

That is equally true today, and it is even more true today that world peace and world good-will are blocked by only 10 or 15 percent of the world's population. That is why efforts to reduce armies have thus far not only failed, but have been met by vastly increased armaments on land and in the air. That is why even efforts to continue the existing limits on naval armaments into the years to come show such little current success.

But the policy of the United States has been clear and consistent. We have sought with earnestness in every possible way to limit world armaments and to attain the peaceful solution of disputes among all Nations.

We have sought by every legitimate means to exert our moral influence against repression, against intolerance, against autocracy and in favor of freedom of expression, equality before the law, religious tolerance and popular rule.

In the field of commerce we have undertaken to encourage a more reasonable interchange of the world's goods. In the field of international finance we have, so far as we are concerned, put an end to dollar diplomacy, to money grabbing, to speculation for the benefit of the powerful and the rich, at the expense of the small and the poor.

As a consistent part of a clear policy, the United States is following a twofold neutrality toward any and all Nations which engage in wars that are not of immediate concern to the Americas. First, we decline to encourage the prosecution of war by permitting belligerents to obtain arms, ammunition or implements of war from the United States. Second, we seek to discourage the use by belligerent Nations of any and all American products calculated to facilitate the prosecution of a war in quantities over and above our normal exports of them in time of peace.

I trust that these objectives thus clearly and unequivocally stated will be carried forward by cooperation between this Congress and the President.

I realize that I have emphasized to you the gravity of the situation which confronts the people of the world. This emphasis is justified because of its importance to civilization and therefore to the United States. Peace is jeopardized by the few and not by the many. Peace is threatened by those who seek selfish power. The world has witnessed similar eras—as in the days when petty kings and feudal barons were changing the map of Europe every fortnight, or when great emperors and great kings were engaged in a mad scramble for colonial empire. We hope that we are not again at the threshold of such an era. But if face it we must, then the United States and the rest of the Americas can play but one role: through a well-ordered neutrality to do naught to encourage the contest, through adequate defense to save ourselves from embroilment and attack, and through example and all legitimate encouragement and assistance to persuade other Nations to return to the ways of peace and good-will.

The evidence before us clearly proves that autocracy in world affairs endangers peace and that such threats do not spring from those Nations devoted to the democratic ideal. If this be true in world affairs, it should have the greatest weight in the determination of domestic policies.

Within democratic Nations the chief concern of the people is to prevent the continuance or the rise of autocratic institutions that beget slavery at home and aggression abroad. Within our borders, as in the world at large, popular opinion is at war with a power-seeking minority.

That is no new thing. It was fought out in the Constitutional Convention of 1787. From time to time since then, the battle has been continued, under Thomas Jefferson, Andrew Jackson, Theodore Roosevelt and Woodrow Wilson.

In these latter years we have witnessed the domination of government by financial and industrial groups, numerically small but politically dominant in the twelve years that succeeded the World War. The present group of which I speak is indeed numerically small and, while it exercises a large influence and has much to say in the world of business, it does not, I am confident, speak the true sentiments of the less articulate but more important elements that constitute real American business.

In March, 1933, I appealed to the Congress of the United States and to the people of the United States in a new effort to restore power to those to whom it rightfully belonged. The response to that appeal resulted in the writing of a new chapter in the history of popular government. You, the members of the Legislative branch, and I, the Executive, contended for and established a new relationship between Government and people.

What were the terms of that new relationship? They were an appeal from the clamor of many private and selfish interests, yes, an appeal from the clamor of partisan interest, to the ideal of the public interest. Government became the representative and the trustee of the public interest. Our aim was to build upon essentially democratic institutions, seeking all the while the adjustment of burdens, the help of the needy, the protection of the weak, the liberation of the exploited and the genuine protection of the people's property.

It goes without saying that to create such an economic constitutional order, more than a single legislative enactment was called for. We, you in the Congress and I as the Executive, had to build upon a broad base. Now, after thirty-four months of work, we contemplate a fairly rounded whole. We have returned the control of the Federal Government to the City of Washington.

To be sure, in so doing, we have invited battle. We have earned the hatred of entrenched greed. The very nature of the problem that we faced made it necessary to drive some people from power and strictly to regulate others. I made that plain when I took the oath of office in March, 1933. I spoke of the practices of the unscrupulous money-changers who stood indicted in the court of public opinion. I spoke of the rulers of the exchanges of mankind's goods, who failed through their own stubbornness and their own incompetence. I said that they had admitted their failure and had abdicated.

Abdicated? Yes, in 1933, but now with the passing of danger they forget their damaging admissions and withdraw their abdication.

They seek the restoration of their selfish power. They offer to lead us back round the same old corner into the same old dreary street.

Yes, there are still determined groups that are intent upon that very thing. Rigorously held up to popular examination, their true character presents itself. They steal the livery of great national constitutional ideals to serve discredited special interests. As guardians and trustees for great groups of individual stockholders they wrongfully seek to carry the property and the interests entrusted to them into the arena of partisan politics. They seek—this minority in business and industry—to control and often do control and use for their own purposes legitimate and highly honored business associations; they engage in vast propaganda to spread fear and discord among the people—they would "gang up" against the people's liberties.

The principle that they would instill into government if they succeed in seizing power is well shown by the principles which many of them have instilled into their own affairs: autocracy toward labor, toward stockholders, toward consumers, toward public sentiment. Autocrats in smaller things, they seek autocracy in bigger things. "By their fruits ye shall know them."

If these gentlemen believe, as they say they believe, that the measures adopted by this Congress and its predecessor, and carried out by this Administration, have hindered rather than promoted recovery, let them be consistent. Let them propose to this Congress the complete repeal of these measures. The way is open to such a proposal.

Let action be positive and not negative. The way is open in the Congress of the United States for an expression of opinion by yeas and nays. Shall we say that values are restored and that the Congress will, therefore, repeal the laws under which we have been bringing them back? Shall we say that because national income has grown with rising prosperity, we shall repeal existing taxes and thereby put off the day of approaching a balanced budget and of starting to reduce the national debt? Shall we abandon the reasonable support and regulation of banking? Shall we restore the dollar to its former gold content?

Shall we say to the farmer, "The prices for your products are in part restored. Now go and hoe your own row?"

Shall we say to the home owners, "We have reduced your rates of interest. We have no further concern with how you keep your home or what you pay for your money. That is your affair?"

Shall we say to the several millions of unemployed citizens who face the very problem of existence, of getting enough to eat, "We will withdraw from giving you work. We will turn you back to the charity of your communities and those men of selfish power who tell you that perhaps they will employ you if the Government leaves them strictly alone?"

Shall we say to the needy unemployed, "Your problem is a local one except that perhaps the Federal Government, as an act of mere generosity, will be willing to pay to your city or to your county a few grudging dollars to help maintain your soup kitchens?"

Shall we say to the children who have worked all day in the factories, "Child labor is a local issue and so are your starvation wages; something to be solved or left unsolved by the jurisdiction of forty-eight States?"

Shall we say to the laborer, "Your right to organize, your relations with your employer have nothing to do with the public interest; if your employer will not even meet with you to discuss your problems and his, that is none of our affair?"

Shall we say to the unemployed and the aged, "Social security lies not within the province of the Federal Government; you must seek relief elsewhere?"

Shall we say to the men and women who live in conditions of squalor in country and in city, "The health and the happiness of you and your children are no concern of ours?"

Shall we expose our population once more by the repeal of laws which protect them against the loss of their honest investments and against the manipulations of dishonest speculators? Shall we abandon the splendid efforts of the Federal Government to raise the health standards of the Nation and to give youth a decent opportunity through such means as the Civilian Conservation Corps?

Members of the Congress, let these challenges be met. If this is what these gentlemen want, let them say so to the Congress of the United States. Let them no longer hide their dissent in a cowardly cloak of generality. Let them define the issue. We have been specific in our affirmative action. Let them be specific in their negative attack.

But the challenge faced by this Congress is more menacing than merely a return to the past—bad as that would be. Our resplendent economic autocracy does not want to return to that individualism of which they prate, even though the advantages under that system went to the ruthless and the strong. They realize that in thirty-four months we have built up new instruments of public power. In the hands of a people's Government this power is wholesome and proper. But in the hands of political puppets of an economic autocracy such power would provide shackles for the liberties of the people. Give them their way and they will take the course of every autocracy of the past—power for themselves, enslavement for the public.

Their weapon is the weapon of fear. I have said, "The only thing we have to fear is fear itself." That is as true today as it was in 1933. But such fear as they instill today is not a natural fear, a normal fear; it is a synthetic, manufactured, poisonous fear that is being spread subtly, expensively and cleverly by the same people who cried in those other days, "Save us, save us, lest we perish."

I am confident that the Congress of the United States well understands the facts and is ready to wage unceasing warfare against those who seek a continuation of that spirit of fear. The carrying out of the laws of the land as enacted by the Congress requires protection until final adjudication by the highest tribunal of the land. The Congress has the right and can find the means to protect its own prerogatives.

We are justified in our present confidence. Restoration of national income, which shows continuing gains for the third successive year, supports the normal and logical policies under which agriculture and industry are returning to full activity. Under these policies we approach a balance of the national budget. National income increases; tax receipts, based on that income, increase without the levying of new taxes. That is why I am able to say to this, the Second Session of the 74th Congress, that it is my belief based on existing laws that no new taxes, over and above the present taxes, are either advisable or necessary.

National income increases; employment increases. Therefore, we can look forward to a reduction in the number of those citizens who are in need. Therefore, also, we can anticipate a reduction in our appropriations for relief.

In the light of our substantial material progress, in the light of the increasing effectiveness of the restoration of popular rule, I recommend to the Congress that we advance; that we do not retreat. I have confidence that you will not fail the people of the Nation whose mandate you have already so faithfully fulfilled.

I repeat, with the same faith and the same determination, my words of March 4, 1933: "We face the arduous days that lie before us in the warm courage of national unity; with a clear consciousness of seeking old and precious moral values; with a clean satisfaction that comes from the stern performance of duty by old and young alike. We aim at the assurance of a rounded and permanent national life. We do not distrust the future of essential democracy."

I cannot better end this message on the state of the Union than by repeating the words of a wise philosopher at whose feet I sat many, many years ago.

"What great crises teach all men whom the example and counsel of the brave inspire is the lesson: Fear not, view all the tasks of life as sacred, have faith in the triumph of the ideal, give daily all that you have to give, be loyal and rejoice whenever you find yourselves part of a great ideal enterprise. You, at this moment, have the honor to belong to a generation whose lips are touched by fire. You live in a land that now enjoys the blessings of peace. But let nothing human be wholly alien to you. The human race now passes through one of its great crises. New ideas, new issues—a new call for men to carry on the work of righteousness, of charity, of courage, of patience, and of loyalty. . . . However memory bring back this moment to your minds, let it be able to say to you: That was a great moment. It was the beginning of a new era. . . . This world in its crisis called for volunteers, for men of faith in life, of patience in service, of charity and of insight. I responded to the call however I could. I volunteered to give myself to my Master—the cause of humane and brave living. I studied, I loved, I labored, unsparingly and hopefully, to be worthy of my generation."

State of the Union Address

Franklin D. Roosevelt

January 6, 1937

Mr. President, Mr. Speaker, Members of the Congress of the United States:

For the first time in our national history a President delivers his Annual Message to a new Congress within a fortnight of the expiration of his term of office. While there is no change in the Presidency this year, change will occur in future years. It is my belief that under this new constitutional practice, the President should in every fourth year, in so far as seems reasonable, review the existing state of our national affairs and outline broad future problems, leaving specific recommendations for future legislation to be made by the President about to be inaugurated.

At this time, however, circumstances of the moment compel me to ask your immediate consideration of: First, measures extending the life of certain authorizations and powers which, under present statutes, expire within a few weeks; second, an addition to the existing Neutrality Act to cover specific points raised by the unfortunate civil strife in Spain; and, third, a deficiency appropriation bill for which I shall submit estimates this week.

In March, 1933, the problems which faced our Nation and which only our national Government had the resources to meet were more serious even than appeared on the surface.

It was not only that the visible mechanism of economic life had broken down. More disturbing was the fact that long neglect of the needs of the underprivileged had brought too many of our people to the verge of doubt as to the successful adaptation of our historic traditions to the complex modern world. In that lay a challenge to our democratic form of Government itself.

Ours was the task to prove that democracy could be made to function in the world of today as effectively as in the simpler world of a hundred years ago. Ours was the task to do more than to argue a theory. The times required the confident answer of performance to those whose instinctive faith in humanity made them want to believe that in the long run democracy would prove superior to more extreme forms of Government as a process of getting action when action was wisdom, without the spiritual sacrifices which those other forms of Government exact.

That challenge we met. To meet it required unprecedented activities under Federal leadership to end abuses, to restore a large measure of material prosperity, to give new faith to millions of our citizens who had been traditionally taught to expect that democracy would provide continuously wider opportunity and continuously greater security in a world where science was continuously making material riches more available to man.

In the many methods of attack with which we met these problems, you and I, by mutual understanding and by determination to cooperate, helped to make democracy succeed by refusing to permit unnecessary disagreement to arise between two of our branches of Government. That spirit of cooperation was able to solve difficulties of extraordinary magnitude and ramification with few important errors, and at a cost cheap when measured by the immediate necessities and the eventual results.

I look forward to a continuance of that cooperation in the next four years. I look forward also to a continuance of the basis of that cooperation— mutual respect for each other's proper sphere of functioning in a democracy which is working well, and a common-sense realization of the need for play in the joints of the machine.

On that basis, it is within the right of the Congress to determine which of the many new activities shall be continued or abandoned, increased or curtailed.

On that same basis, the President alone has the responsibility for their administration. I find that this task of Executive management has reached the point where our administrative machinery needs comprehensive overhauling. I shall, therefore, shortly address the Congress more fully in regard to modernizing and improving the Executive branch of the Government.

That cooperation of the past four years between the Congress and the President has aimed at the fulfillment of a twofold policy: first, economic recovery through many kinds of assistance to agriculture, industry and banking; and, second, deliberate improvement in the personal security and opportunity of the great mass of our people.

The recovery we sought was not to be merely temporary. It was to be a recovery protected from the causes of previous disasters. With that aim in view—to prevent a future similar crisis—you and I joined in a series of enactments—safe banking and sound currency, the guarantee of bank deposits, protection for the investor in securities, the removal of the threat of agricultural surpluses, insistence on collective bargaining, the outlawing of sweat shops, child labor and unfair trade practices, and the beginnings of security for the aged and the worker.

Nor was the recovery we sought merely a purposeless whirring of machinery. It is important, of course, that every man and woman in the country be able to find work, that every factory run, that business and farming as a whole earn profits. But Government in a democratic Nation does not exist solely, or even primarily, for that purpose.

It is not enough that the wheels turn. They must carry us in the direction of a greater satisfaction in life for the average man. The deeper purpose of democratic government is to assist as many of its citizens as possible, especially those who need it most, to improve their conditions of life, to retain all personal liberty which does not adversely affect their neighbors, and to pursue the happiness which comes with security and an opportunity for recreation and culture.

Even with our present recovery we are far from the goal of that deeper purpose. There are far-reaching problems still with us for which democracy must find solutions if it is to consider itself successful.

For example, many millions of Americans still live in habitations which not only fail to provide the physical benefits of modern civilization but breed disease and impair the health of future generations. The menace exists not only in the slum areas of the very large cities, but in many smaller cities as well. It exists on tens of thousands of farms, in varying degrees, in every part of the country.

Another example is the prevalence of an un-American type of tenant farming. I do not suggest that every farm family has the capacity to earn a satisfactory living on its own farm. But many thousands of tenant farmers, indeed most of them, with some financial assistance and with some advice and training, can be made self-supporting on land which can eventually belong to them. The Nation would be wise to offer them that chance instead of permitting them to go along as they do now, year after year, with neither future security as tenants nor hope of ownership of their homes nor expectation of bettering the lot of their children.

Another national problem is the intelligent development of our social security system, the broadening of the services it renders, and practical improvement in its operation. In many Nations where such laws are in effect, success in meeting the expectations of the community has come through frequent amendment of the original statute.

And, of course, the most far-reaching and the most inclusive problem of all is that of unemployment and the lack of economic balance of which unemployment is at once the result and the symptom. The immediate question of adequate relief for the needy unemployed who are capable of performing useful work, I shall discuss with the Congress during the coming months. The broader task of preventing unemployment is a matter of long-range evolutionary policy. To that we must continue to give our best thought and effort. We cannot assume that immediate industrial and commercial activity which mitigates present pressures justifies the national Government at this time in placing the unemployment problem in a filing cabinet of finished business.

Fluctuations in employment are tied to all other wasteful fluctuations in our mechanism of production and distribution. One of these wastes is speculation. In securities or commodities, the larger the volume of speculation, the wider become the upward and downward swings and the more certain the result that in the long run there will be more losses than gains in the underlying wealth of the community.

And, as is now well known to all of us, the same net loss to society comes from reckless overproduction and monopolistic underproduction of natural and manufactured commodities.

Overproduction, underproduction and speculation are three evil sisters who distill the troubles of unsound inflation and disastrous deflation. It is to the interest of the Nation to have Government help private enterprise to gain sound general price levels and to protect those levels from wide perilous fluctuations. We know now that if early in 1931 Government had taken the steps which were taken two and three years later, the depression would never have reached the depths of the beginning of 1933.

Sober second thought confirms most of us in the belief that the broad objectives of the National Recovery Act were sound. We know now that its difficulties arose from the fact that it tried to do too much. For example, it was unwise to expect the same agency to regulate the length of working hours, minimum wages, child labor and collective bargaining on the one hand and the complicated questions of unfair trade practices and business controls on the other.

The statute of N.R.A. has been outlawed. The problems have not. They are still with us.

That decent conditions and adequate pay for labor, and just return for agriculture, can be secured through parallel and simultaneous action by forty-eight States is a proven impossibility. It is equally impossible to obtain curbs on monopoly, unfair trade practices and speculation by State action alone. There are those who, sincerely or insincerely, still cling to State action as a theoretical hope. But experience with actualities makes it clear that Federal laws supplementing State laws are needed to help solve the problems which result from modern invention applied in an industrialized Nation which conducts its business with scant regard to State lines.

During the past year there has been a growing belief that there is little fault to be found with the Constitution of the United States as it stands today. The vital need is not an alteration of our fundamental law, but an increasingly enlightened view with reference to it. Difficulties have grown out of its interpretation; but rightly considered, it can be used as an instrument of progress, and not as a device for prevention of action.

It is worth our while to read and reread the preamble of the Constitution, and Article I thereof which confers the legislative powers upon the Congress of the United States. It is also worth our while to read again the debates in the Constitutional Convention of one hundred and fifty years ago. From such reading, I obtain the very definite thought that the members of that Convention were fully aware that civilization would raise problems for the proposed new Federal Government, which they themselves could not even surmise; and that it was their definite intent and expectation that a liberal interpretation in the years to come would give to the Congress the same relative powers over new national problems as they themselves gave to the Congress over the national problems of their day.

In presenting to the Convention the first basic draft of the Constitution, Edmund Randolph explained that it was the purpose "to insert essential principles only, lest the operation of government should be clogged by rendering those provisions permanent and unalterable which ought to be accommodated to times and events."

With a better understanding of our purposes, and a more intelligent recognition of our needs as a Nation, it is not to be assumed that there will be prolonged failure to bring legislative and judicial action into closer harmony. Means must be found to adapt our legal forms and our judicial interpretation to the actual present national needs of the largest progressive democracy in the modern world.

That thought leads to a consideration of world problems. To go no further back than the beginning of this century, men and women everywhere were seeking conditions of life very different from those which were customary before modern invention and modern industry and modern communications had come into being. The World war, for all of its tragedy, encouraged these demands, and stimulated action to fulfill these new desires.

Many national Governments seemed unable adequately to respond; and, often with the improvident assent of the masses of the people themselves, new forms of government were set up with oligarchy taking the place of democracy. In oligarchies, militarism has leapt forward, while in those Nations which have retained democracy, militarism has waned.

I have recently visited three of our sister Republics in South America. The very cordial receptions with which I was greeted were in tribute to democracy. To me the outstanding observation of that visit was that the masses of the peoples of all the Americas are convinced that the democratic form of government can be made to succeed and do not wish to substitute for it any other form of government. They believe that democracies are best able to cope with the changing problems of modern civilization within themselves, and that democracies are best able to maintain peace among themselves.

The Inter-American Conference, operating on these fundamental principles of democracy, did much to assure peace in this Hemisphere. Existing peace machinery was improved. New instruments to maintain peace and eliminate causes of war were adopted. Wider protection of the interests of the American Republics in the event of war outside the Western Hemisphere was provided. Respect for, and observance of, international treaties and international law were strengthened. Principles of liberal trade policies, as effective aids to the maintenance of peace, were reaffirmed. The intellectual and cultural relationships among American Republics were broadened as a part of the general peace program.

In a world unhappily thinking in terms of war, the representatives of twenty-one Nations sat around a table, in an atmosphere of complete confidence and understanding, sincerely discussing measures for maintaining peace. Here was a great and a permanent achievement directly affecting the lives and security of the two hundred and fifty million human beings who dwell in this Western Hemisphere. Here was an example which must have a wholesome effect upon the rest of the world.

In a very real sense, the Conference in Buenos Aires sent forth a message on behalf of all the democracies of the world to those Nations which live otherwise. Because such other Governments are perhaps more spectacular, it was high time for democracy to assert itself.

Because all of us believe that our democratic form of government can cope adequately with modern problems as they arise, it is patriotic as well as logical for us to prove that we can meet new national needs with new laws consistent with an historic constitutional framework clearly intended to receive liberal and not narrow interpretation.

The United States of America, within itself, must continue the task of making democracy succeed.

In that task the Legislative branch of our Government will, I am confident, continue to meet the demands of democracy whether they relate to the curbing of abuses, the extension of help to those who need help, or the better balancing of our interdependent economies.

So, too, the Executive branch of the Government must move forward in this task, and, at the same time, provide better management for administrative action of all kinds.

The Judicial branch also is asked by the people to do its part in making democracy successful. We do not ask the Courts to call non existent powers into being, but we have a right to expect that conceded powers or those legitimately implied shall be made effective instruments for the common good.

The process of our democracy must not be imperiled by the denial of essential powers of free government.

Your task and mine is not ending with the end of the depression. The people of the United States have made it clear that they expect us to continue our active efforts in behalf of their peaceful advancement.

In that spirit of endeavor and service I greet the 75th Congress at the beginning of this auspicious New Year.

State of the Union Address

Franklin D. Roosevelt

January 3, 1938

Mr. President, Mr. Speaker, Members of the Senate and of the House of Representatives:

In addressing the Congress on the state of the Union present facts and future hazards demand that I speak clearly and earnestly of the causes which underlie events of profound concern to all.

In spite of the determination of this Nation for peace, it has become clear that acts and policies of nations in other parts of the world have far-reaching effects not only upon their immediate neighbors but also on us.

I am thankful that I can tell you that our Nation is at peace. It has been kept at peace despite provocations which in other days, because of their seriousness, could well have engendered war. The people of the United States and the Government of the United States have shown capacity for restraint and a civilized approach to the purposes of peace, while at the same time we maintain the integrity inherent in the sovereignty of 130,000,000 people, lest we weaken or destroy our influence for peace and jeopardize the sovereignty itself.

It is our traditional policy to live at peace with other nations. More than that, we have been among the leaders in advocating the use of pacific methods of discussion and conciliation in international differences. We have striven for the reduction of military forces.

But in a world of high tension and disorder, in a world where stable civilization is actually threatened, it becomes the responsibility of each nation which strives for peace at home and peace with and among others to be strong enough to assure the observance of those fundamentals of peaceful solution of conflicts which are the only ultimate basis for orderly existence.

Resolute in our determination to respect the rights of others, and to command respect for the rights of ourselves, we must keep ourselves adequately strong in self-defense.

There is a trend in the world away from the observance both of the letter and the spirit of treaties. We propose to observe, as we have in the past, our own treaty obligations to the limit; but we cannot be certain of reciprocity on the part of others.

Disregard for treaty obligations seems to have followed the surface trend away from the democratic representative form of government. It would seem, therefore, that world peace through international agreements is most safe in the hands of democratic representative governments—or, in other words, peace is most greatly jeopardized in and by those nations where democracy has been discarded or has never developed.

I have used the words "surface trend," for I still believe that civilized man increasingly insists and in the long run will insist on genuine participation in his own government. Our people believe that over the years democracies of the world will survive, and that democracy will be restored or established in those nations which today know it not. In that faith lies the future peace of mankind.

At home, conditions call for my equal candor. Events of recent months are new proof that we cannot conduct a national government after the practice of 1787, or 1837 or 1887, for the obvious reason that human needs and human desires are infinitely greater, infinitely more difficult to meet than in any previous period in the life of our Republic. Hitherto it has been an acknowledged duty of government to meet these desires and needs: nothing has occurred of late to absolve the Congress, the Courts or the President from that task. It faces us as squarely, as insistently, as in March, 1933.

Much of trouble in our own lifetime has sprung from a long period of inaction—from ignoring what fundamentally was happening to us, and from a time-serving unwillingness to face facts as they forced themselves upon us.

Our national life rests on two nearly equal producing forces, agriculture and industry, each employing about one-third of our citizens. The other third transports and distributes the products of the first two, or performs special services for the whole.

The first great force, agriculture—and with it the production of timber, minerals and other natural resources—went forward feverishly and thoughtlessly until nature rebelled and we saw deserts encroach, floods destroy, trees disappear and soil exhausted.

At the same time we have been discovering that vast numbers of our farming population live in a poverty more abject than that of many of the farmers of Europe whom we are wont to call peasants; that the prices of our products of agriculture are too often dependent on speculation by non-farming groups; and that foreign nations, eager to become self-sustaining or ready to put virgin land under the plough are no longer buying our surpluses of cotton and wheat and lard and tobacco and fruit as they had before.

Since 1933 we have knowingly faced a choice of three remedies. First, to cut our cost of farm production below that of other nations—an obvious impossibility in many crops today unless we revert to human slavery or its equivalent.

Second, to make the government the guarantor of farm prices and the underwriter of excess farm production without limit—a course which would bankrupt the strongest government in the world in a decade.

Third, to place the primary responsibility directly on the farmers themselves, under the principle of majority rule, so that they may decide, with full knowledge of the facts of surpluses, scarcities, world markets and domestic needs, what the planting of each crop should be in order to maintain a reasonably adequate supply which will assure a minimum adequate price under the normal processes of the law of supply and demand.

That means adequacy of supply but not glut. It means adequate reserves against the day of drought. It is shameless misrepresentation to call this a policy of scarcity. It is in truth insurance before the fact, instead of government subsidy after the fact.

Any such plan for the control of excessive surpluses and the speculation they bring has two enemies. There are those well meaning theorists who harp on the inherent right of every free born American to do with his land what he wants—to cultivate it well—or badly; to conserve his timber by cutting only the annual increment thereof—or to strip it clean, let fire burn the slash, and erosion complete the ruin; to raise only one crop—and if that crop fails, to look for food and support from his neighbors or his government.

That, I assert is not an inherent right of citizenship. For if a man farms his land to the waste of the soil or the trees, he destroys not only his own assets but the Nation's assets as well. Or if by his methods he makes himself, year after year, a financial hazard of the community and the government, he becomes not only a social problem but an economic menace. The day has gone by when it could be claimed that government has no interest in such ill-considered practices and no right through representative methods to stop them.

The other group of enemies is perhaps less well-meaning. It includes those who for partisan purposes oppose each and every practical effort to help the situation, and also those who make money from undue fluctuations in crop prices.

I gladly note that measures which seek to initiate a government program for a balanced agriculture are now in conference between the two Houses of the Congress. In their final consideration, I hope for a sound consistent measure which will keep the cost of its administration within the figure of current government expenditures in aid of agriculture. The farmers of this Nation know that a balanced output can be put into effect without excessive cost and with the cooperation of the great majority of them.

If this balance can be created by an all-weather farm program, our farm population will soon be assured of relatively constant purchasing power. From this will flow two other practical results: the consuming public will be protected against excessive food and textile prices, and the industries of the Nation and their workers will find a steadier demand for wares sold to the agricultural third of our people.

To raise the purchasing power of the farmer is, however, not enough. It will not stay raised if we do not also raise the purchasing power of that third of the Nation which receives its income from industrial employment. Millions of industrial workers receive pay so low that they have little buying power. Aside from the undoubted fact that they thereby suffer great human hardship, they are unable to buy adequate food and shelter, to maintain health or to buy their share of manufactured goods.

We have not only seen minimum wage and maximum hour provisions prove their worth economically and socially under government auspices in 1933, 1934 and 1935, but the people of this country, by an overwhelming vote, are in favor of having the Congress—this Congress—put a floor below which industrial wages shall not fall, and a ceiling beyond which the hours of industrial labor shall not rise.

Here again let us analyze the opposition. A part of it is sincere in believing that an effort thus to raise the purchasing power of lowest paid industrial workers is not the business of the Federal Government. Others give "lip service" to a general objective, but do not like any specific measure that is proposed. In both cases it is worth our while to wonder whether some of these opponents are not at heart opposed to any program for raising the wages of the underpaid or reducing the hours of the overworked.

Another group opposes legislation of this type on the ground that cheap labor will help their locality to acquire industries and outside capital, or to retain industries which today are surviving only because of existing low wages and long hours. It has been my thought that, especially during these past five years, this Nation has grown away from local or sectional selfishness and toward national patriotism and unity. I am disappointed by some recent actions and by some recent utterances which sound like the philosophy of half a century ago.

There are many communities in the United States where the average family income is pitifully low. It is in those communities that we find the poorest educational facilities and the worst conditions of health. Why? It is not because they are satisfied to live as they do. It is because those communities have the lowest per capita wealth and income; therefore, the lowest ability to pay taxes; and, therefore, inadequate functioning of local government.

Such communities exist in the East, in the Middle West, in the Far West, and in the South. Those who represent such areas in every part of the country do their constituents ill service by blocking efforts to raise their incomes, their property values and, therefore, their whole scale of living. In the long run, the profits from Child labor, low pay and overwork enure not to the locality or region where they exist but to the absentee owners who have sent their capital into these exploited communities to gather larger profits for themselves. Indeed, new enterprises and new industries which bring permanent wealth will come more readily to those communities which insist on good pay and reasonable hours, for the simple reason that there they will find a greater industrial efficiency and happier workers.

No reasonable person seeks a complete uniformity in wages in every part of the United States; nor does any reasonable person seek an immediate and drastic change from the lowest pay to the highest pay. We are seeking, of course, only legislation to end starvation wages and intolerable hours; more desirable wages are and should continue to be the product of collective bargaining.

Many of those who represent great cities have shown their understanding of the necessity of helping the agricultural third of the Nation. I hope that those who represent constituencies primarily agricultural will not underestimate the importance of extending like aid to the industrial third.

Wage and hour legislation, therefore, is a problem which is definitely before this Congress for action. It is an essential part of economic recovery. It has the support of an overwhelming majority of our people in every walk of life. They have expressed themselves through the ballot box.

Again I revert to the increase of national purchasing power as an underlying necessity of the day. If you increase that purchasing power for the farmers and for the industrial workers, especially for those in both groups who have least of it today, you will increase the purchasing power of the final third of our population—those who transport and distribute the products of farm and factory, and those of the professions who serve all groups. I have tried to make clear to you, and through you to the people of the United States, that this is an urgency which must be met by complete and not by partial action.

If it is met, if the purchasing power of the Nation as a whole—in other words, the total of the Nation's income—can be still further increased, other happy results will flow from such increase.

We have raised the Nation's income from thirty-eight billion dollars in the year 1932 to about sixty-eight billion dollars in the year 1937. Our goal, our objective is to raise it to ninety or one hundred billion dollars.

We have heard much about a balanced budget, and it is interesting to note that many of those who have pleaded for a balanced budget as the sole need now come to me to plead for additional government expenditures at the expense of unbalancing the budget. As the Congress is fully aware, the annual deficit, large for several years, has been declining the last fiscal year and this. The proposed budget for 1939, which I shall shortly send to the Congress, will exhibit a further decrease in the deficit, though not a balance between income and outgo.

To many who have pleaded with me for an immediate balancing of the budget, by a sharp curtailment or even elimination of government functions, I have asked the question: "What present expenditures would you reduce or eliminate?" And the invariable answer has been "that is not my business—I know nothing of the details, but I am sure that it could be done." That is not what you or I would call helpful citizenship.

On only one point do most of them have a suggestion. They think that relief for the unemployed by the giving of work is wasteful, and when I pin them down I discover that at heart they are actually in favor of substituting a dole in place of useful work. To that neither I nor, I am confident, the Senators and Representatives in the Congress will ever consent.

I am as anxious as any banker or industrialist or business man or investor or economist that the budget of the United States Government be brought into balance as quickly as possible. But I lay down certain conditions which seem reasonable and which I believe all should accept.

The first condition is that we continue the policy of not permitting any needy American who can and is willing to work to starve because the Federal Government does not provide the work.

The second is that the Congress and the Executive join hands in eliminating or curtailing any Federal activity which can be eliminated or curtailed or even postponed without harming necessary government functions or the safety of the Nation from a national point of view.

The third is to raise the purchasing power of the Nation to the point that the taxes on this purchasing power—or, in other words, on the Nation's income—will be sufficient to meet the necessary expenditures of the national government.

I have hitherto stated that, in my judgment, the expenditures of the national government cannot be cut much below seven billion dollars a year without destroying essential functions or letting people starve. That sum can be raised and will be cheerfully provided by the American people, if we can increase the Nation's income to a point well beyond the present level.

This does not mean that as the Nation's income goes up the Federal expenditures should rise in proportion. On the contrary, the Congress and the Executive should use every effort to hold the normal Federal expenditures to approximately the present level, thus making it possible, with an increase in the Nation's income and the resulting increase in tax receipts, not only to balance future budgets but to reduce the debt.

In line with this policy fall my former recommendations for the reorganization and improvement of the administrative structure of the government, both for immediate Executive needs and for the planning of future national needs. I renew those recommendations.

In relation to tax changes, three things should be kept in mind. First, the total sum to be derived by the Federal Treasury must not be decreased as a result of any changes in schedules. Second, abuses by individuals or corporations designed to escape tax-paying by using various methods of doing business, corporate and otherwise—abuses which we have sought, with great success, to end—must not be restored. Third, we should rightly change certain provisions where they are proven to work definite hardship, especially on the small business men of the Nation. But, speculative income should not be favored over earned income.

It is human nature to argue that this or that tax is responsible for every ill. It is human nature on the part of those who pay graduated taxes to attack all taxes based on the principle of ability to pay. These are the same complainants who for a generation blocked the imposition of a graduated income tax. They are the same complainants who would impose the type of flat sales tax which places the burden of government more on those least able to pay and less on those most able to pay.

Our conclusion must be that while proven hardships should be corrected, they should not be corrected in such a way as to restore abuses already terminated or to shift a greater burden to the less fortunate.

This subject leads naturally into the wider field of the public attitude toward business. The objective of increasing the purchasing power of the farming third, the industrial third and the service third of our population presupposes the cooperation of what we call capital and labor.

Capital is essential; reasonable earnings on capital are essential; but misuse of the powers of capital or selfish suspension of the employment of capital must be ended, or the capitalistic system will destroy itself through its own abuses.

The overwhelming majority of business men and bankers intend to be good citizens. Only a small minority have displayed poor citizenship by engaging in practices which are dishonest or definitely harmful to society. This statement is straightforward and true. No person in any responsible place in the Government of the United States today has ever taken any position contrary to it.

But, unfortunately for the country, when attention is called to, or attack is made on specific misuses of capital, there has been a deliberate purpose on the part of the condemned minority to distort the criticism into an attack on all capital. That is wilful deception but it does not long deceive.

If attention is called to, or attack made on, certain wrongful business practices, there are those who are eager to call it "an attack on all business." That, too, is wilful deception that will not long deceive. Let us consider certain facts:

There are practices today which most people believe should be ended. They include tax avoidance through corporate and other methods, which I have previously mentioned; excessive capitalization, investment write-ups and security manipulations; price rigging and collusive bidding in defiance of the spirit of the antitrust laws by methods which baffle prosecution under the present statutes. They include high-pressure salesmanship which creates cycles of overproduction within given industries and consequent recessions in production until such time as the surplus is consumed; the use of patent laws to enable larger corporations to maintain high prices and withhold from the public the advantages of the progress of science; unfair competition which drives the smaller producer out of business locally, regionally or even on a national scale; intimidation of local or state government to prevent the enactment of laws for the protection of labor by threatening to move elsewhere; the shifting of actual production from one locality or region to another in pursuit of the cheapest wage scale.

The enumeration of these abuses does not mean that business as a whole is guilty of them. Again, it is deception that will not long deceive to tell the country that an attack on these abuses is an attack on business.

Another group of problems affecting business, which cannot be termed specific abuses, gives us food for grave thought about the future. Generically such problems arise out of the concentration of economic control to the detriment of the body politic—control of other people's money, other people's labor, other people's lives.

In many instances such concentrations cannot be justified on the ground of operating efficiency, but have been created for the sake of securities profits, financial control, the suppression of competition and the ambition for power over others. In some lines of industry a very small numerical group is in such a position of influence that its actions are of necessity followed by the other units operating in the same field.

That such influences operate to control banking and finance is equally true, in spite of the many efforts, through Federal legislation, to take such control out of the hands of a small group. We have but to talk with hundreds of small bankers throughout the United States to realize that irrespective of local conditions, they are compelled in practice to accept the policies laid down by a small number of the larger banks in the Nation. The work undertaken by Andrew Jackson and Woodrow Wilson is not finished yet.

The ownership of vast properties or the organization of thousands of workers creates a heavy obligation of public service. The power should not be sought or sanctioned unless the responsibility is accepted as well. The man who seeks freedom from such responsibility in the name of individual liberty is either fooling himself or trying to cheat his fellow men. He wants to eat the fruits of orderly society without paying for them.

As a Nation we have rejected any radical revolutionary program. For a permanent correction of grave weaknesses in our economic system we have relied on new applications of old democratic processes. It is not necessary to recount what has been accomplished in preserving the homes and livelihood of millions of workers on farms and in cities, in reconstructing a sound banking and credit system, in reviving trade and industry, in reestablishing security of life and property. All we need today is to look upon the fundamental, sound economic conditions to know that this business recession causes more perplexity than fear on the part of most people and to contrast our prevailing mental attitude with the terror and despair of five years ago.

Furthermore, we have a new moral climate in America. That means that we ask business and finance to recognize that fact, to cure such inequalities as they can cure without legislation but to join their government in the enactment of legislation where the ending of abuses and the steady functioning of our economic system calls for government assistance. The Nation has no obligation to make America safe either for incompetent business men or for business men who fail to note the trend of the times and continue the use of machinery of economics and practices of finance as outworn as the cotton spindle of 1870.

Government can be expected to cooperate in every way with the business of the Nation provided the component parts of business abandon practices which do not belong to this day and age, and adopt price and production policies appropriate to the times.

In regard to the relationship of government to certain processes of business, to which I have referred, it seems clear to me that existing laws undoubtedly require reconstruction. I expect, therefore, to address the Congress in a special message on this subject, and I hope to have the help of business in the efforts of government to help business.

I have spoken of labor as another essential in the three great groups of the population in raising the Nation's income. Definite strides in collective bargaining have been made and the right of labor to organize has been nationally accepted. Nevertheless in the evolution of the process difficult situations have arisen in localities and among groups. Unfortunate divisions relating to jurisdiction among the workers themselves have retarded production within given industries and have, therefore, affected related industries. The construction of homes and other buildings has been hindered in some localities not only by unnecessarily high prices for materials but also by certain hourly wage scales.

For economic and social reasons our principal interest for the near future lies along two lines: first, the immediate desirability of increasing the wages of the lowest paid groups in all industry; and, second, in thinking in terms of regularizing the work of the individual worker more greatly through the year—in other words, in thinking more in terms of the worker's total pay for a period of a whole year rather than in terms of his remuneration by the hour or by the day.

In the case of labor as in the case of capital, misrepresentation of the policy of the government of the United States is deception which will not long deceive. In both cases we seek cooperation. In every case power and responsibility must go hand in hand.

I have spoken of economic causes which throw the Nation's income out of balance; I have spoken of practices and abuses which demand correction through the cooperation of capital and labor with the government. But no government can help the destinies of people who insist in putting sectional and class consciousness ahead of general weal. There must be proof that sectional and class interests are prepared more greatly than they are today to be national in outlook.

A government can punish specific acts of spoliation; but no government can conscript cooperation. We have improved some matters by way of remedial legislation. But where in some particulars that legislation has failed we cannot be sure whether it fails because some of its details are unwise or because it is being sabotaged. At any rate, we hold our objectives and our principles to be sound. We will never go back on them.

Government has a final responsibility for the well-being of its citizenship. If private cooperative endeavor fails to provide work for willing hands and relief for the unfortunate, those suffering hardship from no fault of their own have a right to call upon the Government for aid; and a government worthy of its name must make fitting response.

It is the opportunity and the duty of all those who have faith in democratic methods as applied in industry, in agriculture and in business, as well as in the field of politics, to do their utmost to cooperate with government—without regard to political affiliation, special interests or economic prejudices—in whatever program may be sanctioned by the chosen representatives of the people.

That presupposes on the part of the representatives of the people, a program, its enactment and its administration.

Not because of the pledges of party programs alone, not because of the clear policies of the past five years, but chiefly because of the need of national unity in ending mistakes of the past and meeting the necessities of today, we must carry on. I do not propose to let the people down.

I am sure the Congress of the United States will not let the people down.

State of the Union Address

Franklin D. Roosevelt

January 4, 1939

Mr. Vice President, Mr. Speaker, Members of the Senate and the Congress:

In Reporting on the state of the nation, I have felt it necessary on previous occasions to advise the Congress of disturbance abroad and of the need of putting our own house in order in the face of storm signals from across the seas. As this Seventy-sixth Congress opens there is need for further warning.

A war which threatened to envelop the world in flames has been averted; but it has become increasingly clear that world peace is not assured.

All about us rage undeclared wars—military and economic. All about us grow more deadly armaments—military and economic. All about us are threats of new aggression military and economic.

Storms from abroad directly challenge three institutions indispensable to Americans, now as always. The first is religion. It is the source of the other two—democracy and international good faith.

Religion, by teaching man his relationship to God, gives the individual a sense of his own dignity and teaches him to respect himself by respecting his neighbors.

Democracy, the practice of self-government, is a covenant among free men to respect the rights and liberties of their fellows.

International good faith, a sister of democracy, springs from the will of civilized nations of men to respect the rights and liberties of other nations of men.

In a modern civilization, all three—religion, democracy and international good faith—complement and support each other.

Where freedom of religion has been attacked, the attack has come from sources opposed to democracy. Where democracy has been overthrown, the spirit of free worship has disappeared. And where religion and democracy have vanished, good faith and reason in international affairs have given way to strident ambition and brute force.

An ordering of society which relegates religion, democracy and good faith among nations to the background can find no place within it for the ideals of the Prince of Peace. The United States rejects such an ordering, and retains its ancient faith.

There comes a time in the affairs of men when they must prepare to defend, not their homes alone, but the tenets of faith and humanity on which their churches, their governments and their very civilization are founded. The defense of religion, of democracy and of good faith among nations is all the same fight. To save one we must now make up our minds to save all.

We know what might happen to us of the United States if the new philosophies of force were to encompass the other continents and invade our own. We, no more than other nations, can afford to be surrounded by the enemies of our faith and our humanity. Fortunate it is, therefore, that in this Western Hemisphere we have, under a common ideal of democratic government, a rich diversity of resources and of peoples functioning together in mutual respect and peace.

That Hemisphere, that peace, and that ideal we propose to do our share in protecting against storms from any quarter. Our people and our resources are pledged to secure that protection. From that determination no American flinches.

This by no means implies that the American Republics disassociate themselves from the nations of other continents. It does not mean the Americas against the rest of the world. We as one of the Republics reiterate our willingness to help the cause of world peace. We stand on our historic offer to take counsel with all other nations of the world to the end that aggression among them be terminated, that the race of armaments cease and that commerce be renewed.

But the world has grown so small and weapons of attack so swift that no nation can be safe in its will to peace so long as any other powerful nation refuses to settle its grievances at the council table.

For if any government bristling with implements of war insists on policies of force, weapons of defense give the only safety.

In our foreign relations we have learned from the past what not to do. From new wars we have learned what we must do.

We have learned that effective timing of defense, and the distant points from which attacks may be launched are completely different from what they were twenty years ago.

We have learned that survival cannot be guaranteed by arming after the attack begins—for there is new range and speed to offense.

We have learned that long before any overt military act, aggression begins with preliminaries of propaganda, subsidized penetration, the loosening of ties of good will, the stirring of prejudice and the incitement to disunion.

We have learned that God-fearing democracies of the world which observe the sanctity of treaties and good faith in their dealings with other nations cannot safely be indifferent to international lawlessness anywhere. They cannot forever let pass, without effective protest, acts of aggression against sister nations—acts which automatically undermine all of us.

Obviously they must proceed along practical, peaceful lines. But the mere fact that we rightly decline to intervene with arms to prevent acts of aggression does not mean that we must act as if there were no aggression at all. Words may be futile, but war is not the only means of commanding a decent respect for the opinions of mankind. There are many methods short of war, but stronger and more effective than mere words, of bringing home to aggressor governments the aggregate sentiments of our own people.

At the very least, we can and should avoid any action, or any lack of action, which will encourage, assist or build up an aggressor. We have learned that when we deliberately try to legislate neutrality, our neutrality laws may operate unevenly and unfairly—may actually give aid to an aggressor and deny it to the victim. The instinct of self-preservation should warn us that we ought not to let that happen any more.

And we have learned something else—the old, old lesson that probability of attack is mightily decreased by the assurance of an ever ready defense. Since 1931, nearly eight years ago, world events of thunderous import have moved with lightning speed. During these eight years many of our people clung to the hope that the innate decency of mankind would protect the unprepared who showed their innate trust in mankind. Today we are all wiser—and sadder.

Under modern conditions what we mean by "adequate defense"—a policy subscribed to by all of us—must be divided into three elements. First, we must have armed forces and defenses strong enough to ward off sudden attack against strategic positions and key facilities essential to ensure sustained resistance and ultimate victory. Secondly, we must have the organization and location of those key facilities so that they may be immediately utilized and rapidly expanded to meet all needs without danger of serious interruption by enemy attack.

In the course of a few days I shall send you a special message making recommendations for those two essentials of defense against danger which we cannot safely assume will not come.

If these first two essentials are reasonably provided for, we must be able confidently to invoke the third element, the underlying strength of citizenship—the self-confidence, the ability, the imagination and the devotion that give the staying power to see things through.

A strong and united nation may be destroyed if it is unprepared against sudden attack. But even a nation well armed and well organized from a strictly military standpoint may, after a period of time, meet defeat if it is unnerved by self-distrust, endangered by class prejudice, by dissension between capital and labor, by false economy and by other unsolved social problems at home.

In meeting the troubles of the world we must meet them as one people—with a unity born of the fact that for generations those who have come to our shores, representing many kindreds and tongues, have been welded by common opportunity into a united patriotism. If another form of government can present a united front in its attack on a democracy, the attack must and will be met by a united democracy. Such a democracy can and must exist in the United States.

A dictatorship may command the full strength of a regimented nation. But the united strength of a democratic nation can be mustered only when its people, educated by modern standards to know what is going on and where they are going, have conviction that they are receiving as large a share of opportunity for development, as large a share of material success and of human dignity, as they have a right to receive.

Our nation's program of social and economic reform is therefore a part of defense, as basic as armaments themselves.

Against the background of events in Europe, in Africa and in Asia during these recent years, the pattern of what we have accomplished since 1933 appears in even clearer focus.

For the first time we have moved upon deep-seated problems affecting our national strength and have forged national instruments adequate to meet them.

Consider what the seemingly piecemeal struggles of these six years add up to in terms of realistic national preparedness.

We are conserving and developing natural resources—land, water power, forests.

We are trying to provide necessary food, shelter and medical care for the health of our population.

We are putting agriculture—our system of food and fibre supply—on a sounder basis.

We are strengthening the weakest spot in our system of industrial supply— its long smouldering labor difficulties.

We have cleaned up our credit system so that depositor and investor alike may more readily and willingly make their capital available for peace or war.

We are giving to our youth new opportunities for work and education.

We have sustained the morale of all the population by the dignified recognition of our obligations to the aged, the helpless and the needy.

Above all, we have made the American people conscious of their interrelationship and their interdependence. They sense a common destiny and a common need of each other. Differences of occupation, geography, race and religion no longer obscure the nation's fundamental unity in thought and in action.

We have our difficulties, true—but we are a wiser and a tougher nation than we were in 1929, or in 1932.

Never have there been six years of such far-flung internal preparedness in our history. And this has been done without any dictator's power to command, without conscription of labor or confiscation of capital, without concentration camps and without a scratch on freedom of speech, freedom of the press or the rest of the Bill of Rights.

We see things now that we could not see along the way. The tools of government which we had in 1933 are outmoded. We have had to forge new tools for a new role of government operating in a democracy—a role of new responsibility for new needs and increased responsibility for old needs, long neglected.

Some of these tools had to be roughly shaped and still need some machining down. Many of those who fought bitterly against the forging of these new tools welcome their use today. The American people, as a whole, have accepted them. The Nation looks to the Congress to improve the new machinery which we have permanently installed, provided that in the process the social usefulness of the machinery is not destroyed or impaired.

All of us agree that we should simplify and improve laws if experience and operation clearly demonstrate the need. For instance, all of us want better provision for our older people under our social security legislation. For the medically needy we must provide better care.

Most of us agree that for the sake of employer and employee alike we must find ways to end factional labor strife and employer-employee disputes.

Most of us recognize that none of these tools can be put to maximum effectiveness unless the executive processes of government are revamped—reorganized, if you will—into more effective combination. And even after such reorganization it will take time to develop administrative personnel and experience in order to use our new tools with a minimum of mistakes. The Congress, of course, needs no further information on this.

With this exception of legislation to provide greater government efficiency, and with the exception of legislation to ameliorate our railroad and other transportation problems, the past three Congresses have met in part or in whole the pressing needs of the new order of things.

We have now passed the period of internal conflict in the launching of our program of social reform. Our full energies may now be released to invigorate the processes of recovery in order to preserve our reforms, and to give every man and woman who wants to work a real job at a living wage.

But time is of paramount importance. The deadline of danger from within and from without is not within our control. The hour-glass may be in the hands of other nations. Our own hour-glass tells us that we are off on a race to make democracy work, so that we may be efficient in peace and therefore secure in national defense.

This time element forces us to still greater efforts to attain the full employment of our labor and our capital.

The first duty of our statesmanship is to bring capital and man-power together.

Dictatorships do this by main force. By using main force they apparently succeed at it—for the moment. However we abhor their methods, we are compelled to admit that they have obtained substantial utilization of all their material and human resources. Like it or not, they have solved, for a time at least, the problem of idle men and idle capital. Can we compete with them by boldly seeking methods of putting idle men and idle capital together and, at the same time, remain within our American way of life, within the Bill of Rights, and within the bounds of what is, from our point of view, civilization itself?

We suffer from a great unemployment of capital. Many people have the idea that as a nation we are overburdened with debt and are spending more than we can afford. That is not so. Despite our Federal Government expenditures the entire debt of our national economic system, public and private together, is no larger today than it was in 1929, and the interest thereon is far less than it was in 1929.

The object is to put capital—private as well as public—to work.

We want to get enough capital and labor at work to give us a total turnover of business, a total national income, of at least eighty billion dollars a year. At that figure we shall have a substantial reduction of unemployment; and the Federal Revenues will be sufficient to balance the current level of cash expenditures on the basis of the existing tax structure. That figure can be attained, working within the framework of our traditional profit system.

The factors in attaining and maintaining that amount of national income are many and complicated.

They include more widespread understanding among business men of many changes which world conditions and technological improvements have brought to our economy over the last twenty years—changes in the interrelationship of price and volume and employment, for example—changes of the kind in which business men are now educating themselves through excellent opportunities like the so-called "monopoly investigation."

They include a perfecting of our farm program to protect farmers' income and consumers' purchasing power from alternate risks of crop gluts and crop shortages.

They include wholehearted acceptance of new standards of honesty in our financial markets.

They include reconcilement of enormous, antagonistic interests—some of them long in litigation—in the railroad and general transportation field.

They include the working out of new techniques—private, state and federal—to protect the public interest in and to develop wider markets for electric power.

They include a revamping of the tax relationships between federal, state and local units of government, and consideration of relatively small tax increases to adjust inequalities without interfering with the aggregate income of the American people.

They include the perfecting of labor organization and a universal ungrudging attitude by employers toward the labor movement, until there is a minimum of interruption of production and employment because of disputes, and acceptance by labor of the truth that the welfare of labor itself depends on increased balanced out-put of goods.

To be immediately practical, while proceeding with a steady evolution in the solving of these and like problems, we must wisely use instrumentalities, like Federal investment, which are immediately available to us.

Here, as elsewhere, time is the deciding factor in our choice of remedies.

Therefore, it does not seem logical to me, at the moment we seek to increase production and consumption, for the Federal Government to consider a drastic curtailment of its own investments.

The whole subject of government investing and government income is one which may be approached in two different ways.

The first calls for the elimination of enough activities of government to bring the expenses of government immediately into balance with income of government. This school of thought maintains that because our national income this year is only sixty billion dollars, ours is only a sixty billion dollar country; that government must treat it as such; and that without the help of government, it may some day, somehow, happen to become an eighty billion dollar country.

If the Congress decides to accept this point of view, it will logically have to reduce the present functions or activities of government by one-third. Not only will the Congress have to accept the responsibility for such reduction; but the Congress will have to determine which activities are to be reduced.

Certain expenditures we cannot possibly reduce at this session, such as the interest on the public debt. A few million dollars saved here or there in the normal or in curtailed work of the old departments and commissions will make no great saving in the Federal budget. Therefore, the Congress would have to reduce drastically some of certain large items, very large items, such as aids to agriculture and soil conservation, veterans' pensions, flood control, highways, waterways and other public works, grants for social and health security, Civilian Conservation Corps activities, relief for the unemployed, or national defense itself.

The Congress alone has the power to do all this, as it is the appropriating branch of the government.

The other approach to the question of government spending takes the position that this Nation ought not to be and need not be only a sixty billion dollar nation; that at this moment it has the men and the resources sufficient to make it at least an eighty billion dollar nation. This school of thought does not believe that it can become an eighty billion dollar nation in the near future if government cuts its operations by one-third. It is convinced that if we were to try it, we would invite disaster—and that we would not long remain even a sixty billion dollar nation. There are many complicated factors with which we have to deal, but we have learned that it is unsafe to make abrupt reductions at any time in our net expenditure program.

By our common sense action of resuming government activities last spring, we have reversed a recession and started the new rising tide of prosperity and national income which we are now just beginning to enjoy.

If government activities are fully maintained, there is a good prospect of our becoming an eighty billion dollar country in a very short time. With such a national income, present tax laws will yield enough each year to balance each year's expenses.

It is my conviction that down in their hearts the American public—industry, agriculture, finance—want this Congress to do whatever needs to be done to raise our national income to eighty billion dollars a year.

Investing soundly must preclude spending wastefully. To guard against opportunist appropriations, I have on several occasions addressed the Congress on the importance of permanent long-range planning. I hope, therefore, that following my recommendation of last year, a permanent agency will be set up and authorized to report on the urgency and desirability of the various types of government investment.

Investment for prosperity can be made in a democracy.

I hear some people say, "This is all so complicated. There are certain advantages in a dictatorship. It gets rid of labor trouble, of unemployment, of wasted motion and of having to do your own thinking."

My answer is, "Yes, but it also gets rid of some other things which we Americans intend very definitely to keep—and we still intend to do our own thinking."

It will cost us taxes and the voluntary risk of capital to attain some of the practical advantages which other forms of government have acquired.

Dictatorship, however, involves costs which the American people will never pay: The cost of our spiritual values. The cost of the blessed right of being able to say what we please. The cost of freedom of religion. The cost of seeing our capital confiscated. The cost of being cast into a concentration camp. The cost of being afraid to walk down the street with the wrong neighbor. The cost of having our children brought up, not as free and dignified human beings, but as pawns molded and enslaved by a machine.

If the avoidance of these costs means taxes on my income; if avoiding these costs means taxes on my estate at death, I would bear those taxes willingly as the price of my breathing and my children breathing the free air of a free country, as the price of a living and not a dead world.

Events abroad have made it increasingly clear to the American people that dangers within are less to be feared than dangers from without. If, therefore, a solution of this problem of idle men and idle capital is the price of preserving our liberty, no formless selfish fears can stand in the way.

Once I prophesied that this generation of Americans had a rendezvous with destiny. That prophecy comes true. To us much is given; more is expected.

This generation will "nobly save or meanly lose the last best hope of earth. . . . The way is plain, peaceful, generous, just—a way which if followed the world will forever applaud and God must forever bless."

State of the Union Address

Franklin D. Roosevelt

January 3, 1940

Mr. Vice President, Mr. Speaker, Members of the Senate and the House of Representatives:

I wish each and every one of you a very happy New Year.

As the Congress reassembles, the impact of war abroad makes it natural to approach "the state of the union" through a discussion of foreign affairs.

But it is important that those who hear and read this message should in no way confuse that approach with any thought that our Government is abandoning, or even overlooking, the great significance of its domestic policies.

The social and economic forces which have been mismanaged abroad until they have resulted in revolution, dictatorship and war are the same as those which we here are struggling to adjust peacefully at home.

You are well aware that dictatorships—and the philosophy of force that justifies and accompanies dictatorships—have originated in almost every case in the necessity for drastic action to improve internal conditions in places where democratic action for one reason or another has failed to respond to modern needs and modern demands.

It was with far-sighted wisdom that the framers of our Constitution brought together in one magnificent phrase three great concepts—"common defense," "general welfare" and "domestic tranquility."

More than a century and a half later we, who are here today, still believe with them that our best defense is the promotion of our general welfare and domestic tranquillity.

In previous messages to the Congress I have repeatedly warned that, whether we like it or not, the daily lives of American citizens will, of necessity, feel the shock of events on other continents. This is no longer mere theory; because it has been definitely proved to us by the facts of yesterday and today.

To say that the domestic well-being of one hundred and thirty million Americans is deeply affected by the well-being or the ill-being of the populations of other nations is only to recognize in world affairs the truth that we all accept in home affairs.

If in any local unit—a city, county, State or region—low standards of living are permitted to continue, the level of the civilization of the entire nation will be pulled downward.

The identical principle extends to the rest of the civilized world. But there are those who wishfully insist, in innocence or ignorance or both, that the United States of America as a self-contained unit can live happily and prosperously, its future secure, inside a high wall of isolation while, outside, the rest of Civilization and the commerce and culture of mankind are shattered.

I can understand the feelings of those who warn the nation that they will never again consent to the sending of American youth to fight on the soil of

Europe. But, as I remember, nobody has asked them to consent—for nobody expects such an undertaking.

The overwhelming majority of our fellow citizens do not abandon in the slightest their hope and their expectation that the United States will not become involved in military participation in these wars.

I can also understand the wishfulness of those who oversimplify the whole situation by repeating that all we have to do is to mind our own business and keep the nation out of war. But there is a vast difference between keeping out of war and pretending that this war is none of our business.

We do not have to go to war with other nations, but at least we can strive with other nations to encourage the kind of peace that will lighten the troubles of the world, and by so doing help our own nation as well.

I ask that all of us everywhere think things through with the single aim of how best to serve the future of our own nation. I do not mean merely its future relationship with the outside world. I mean its domestic future as well—the work, the security, the prosperity, the happiness, the life of all the boys and girls in the United States, as they are inevitably affected by such world relationships. For it becomes clearer and clearer that the future world will be a shabby and dangerous place to live in—yes, even for Americans to live in—if it is ruled by force in the hands of a few.

Already the crash of swiftly moving events over the earth has made us all think with a longer view. Fortunately, that thinking cannot be controlled by partisanship. The time is long past when any political party or any particular group can curry or capture public favor by labeling itself the "peace party" or the "peace bloc." That label belongs to the whole United States and to every right thinking man, woman and child within it.

For out of all the military and diplomatic turmoil, out of all the propaganda, and counter-propaganda of the present conflicts, there are two facts which stand out, and which the whole world acknowledges.

The first is that never before has the Government of the United States of America done so much as in our recent past to establish and maintain the policy of the Good Neighbor with its sister nations.

The second is that in almost every nation in the world today there is a true public belief that the United States has been, and will continue to be, a potent and active factor in seeking the reestablishment of world peace.

In these recent years we have had a clean record of peace and good-will. It is an open book that cannot be twisted or defamed. It is a record that must be continued and enlarged.

So I hope that Americans everywhere will work out for themselves the several alternatives which lie before world civilization, which necessarily includes our own.

We must look ahead and see the possibilities for our children if the rest of the world comes to be dominated by concentrated force alone—even though today we are a very great and a very powerful nation.

We must look ahead and see the effect on our own future if all the small nations of the world have their independence snatched from them or become mere appendages to relatively vast and powerful military systems.

We must look ahead and see the kind of lives our children would have to lead if a large part of the rest of the world were compelled to worship a god imposed by a military ruler, or were forbidden to worship God at all; if the rest of the world were forbidden to read and hear the facts—the daily news of their own and other nations—if they were deprived of the truth that makes men free.

We must look ahead and see the effect on our future generations if world trade is controlled by any nation or group of nations which sets up that control through military force.

It is, of course, true that the record of past centuries includes destruction of many small nations, the enslavement of peoples, and the building of empires on the foundation of force. But wholly apart from the greater international morality which we seek today, we recognize the practical fact that with modern weapons and modern conditions, modern man can no longer lead a civilized life if we are to go back to the practice of wars and conquests of the seventeenth and eighteenth centuries.

Summing up this need of looking ahead, and in words of common sense and good American citizenship. I hope that we shall have fewer American ostriches in our midst. It is not good for the ultimate health of ostriches to bury their heads in the sand.

Only an ostrich would look upon these wars through the eyes of cynicism or ridicule.

Of course, the peoples of other nations have the right to choose their own form of Government. But we in this nation still believe that such choice should be predicated on certain freedoms which we think are essential everywhere. We know that we ourselves shall never be wholly safe at home unless other governments recognize such freedoms.

Twenty-one American Republics, expressing the will of two hundred and fifty million people to preserve peace and freedom in this Hemisphere, are displaying a unanimity of ideals and practical relationships which gives hope that what is being done here can be done on other continents. We in all the Americas are coming to the realization that we can retain our respective nationalities without, at the same time, threatening the national existence of our neighbors.

Such truly friendly relationships, for example, permit us to follow our own domestic policies with reference to our agricultural products, while at the same time we have the privilege of trying to work out mutual assistance arrangements for a world distribution of world agricultural surpluses.

And we have been able to apply the same simple principle to many manufactured products—surpluses of which must be sold in the world export markets if we intend to continue a high level of production and employment.

For many years after the World War blind economic selfishness in most countries, including our own, resulted in a destructive mine-field of trade restrictions which blocked the channels of commerce among nations. Indeed, this policy was one of the contributing causes of existing wars. It dammed up vast unsalable surpluses, helping to bring about unemployment and suffering in the United States and everywhere else.

To point the way to break up that log-jam our Trade Agreements Act was passed—based upon a policy of equality of treatment among nations and of mutually profitable arrangements of trade.

It is not correct to infer that legislative powers have been transferred from the Congress to the Executive Branch of the Government. Everyone recognizes that general tariff legislation is a Congressional function; but we know that, because of the stupendous task involved in the fashioning and the passing of a general tariff law, it is advisable to provide at times of emergency some flexibility to make the general law adjustable to quickly changing conditions.

We are in such a time today. Our present trade agreement method provides a temporary flexibility and is, therefore, practical in the best sense. It should be kept alive to serve our trade interests—agricultural and industrial—in many valuable ways during the existing wars.

But what is more important, the Trade Agreements Act should be extended as an indispensable part of the foundation of any stable and enduring peace.

The old conditions of world trade made for no enduring peace; and when the time comes, the United States must use its influence to open up the trade channels of the world, in all nations, in order that no one nation need feel compelled in later days to seek by force of arms what it can well gain by peaceful conference. For that purpose, too, we need the Trade Agreements Act even more today than when it was passed.

I emphasize the leadership which this nation can take when the time comes for a renewal of world peace. Such an influence will be greatly weakened if this Government becomes a dog in the manger of trade selfishness.

The first President of the United States warned us against entangling foreign alliances. The present President of the United States subscribes to and follows that precept.

I hope that most of you will agree that trade cooperation with the rest of the world does not violate that precept in any way.

Even as through these trade agreements we prepare to cooperate in a world that wants peace, we must likewise be prepared to take care of ourselves if the world cannot attain peace.

For several years past we have been compelled to strengthen our own national defense. That has created a very large portion of our Treasury deficits. This year in the light of continuing world uncertainty, I am asking the Congress for Army and Navy increases which are based not on panic but on common sense. They are not as great as enthusiastic alarmists seek. They are not as small as unrealistic persons claiming superior private information would demand.

As will appear in the annual budget tomorrow, the only important increase in any part of the budget is the estimate for national defense. Practically all other important items show a reduction. But you know, you can't eat your cake and have it too. Therefore, in the hope that we can continue in these days of increasing economic prosperity to reduce the Federal deficit, I am asking the Congress to levy sufficient additional taxes to meet the emergency spending for national defense.

Behind the Army and Navy, of course, lies our ultimate line of defense—"the general welfare" of our people. We cannot report, despite all the progress that we have made in our domestic problems—despite the fact that production is back to 1929 levels—that all our problems are solved. The fact of unemployment of millions of men and women remains a symptom of a number of difficulties in our economic system not yet adjusted.

While the number of the unemployed has decreased very greatly, while their immediate needs for food and clothing—as far as the Federal Government is concerned—have been largely met, while their morale has been kept alive by giving them useful public work, we have not yet found a way to employ the surplus of our labor which the efficiency of our industrial processes has created.

We refuse the European solution of using the unemployed to build up excessive armaments which eventually result in dictatorships and war. We encourage an American way—through an increase of national income which is the only way we can be sure will take up the slack. Much progress has been made; much remains to be done.

We recognize that we must find an answer in terms of work and opportunity.

The unemployment problem today has become very definitely a problem of youth as well as of age. As each year has gone by hundreds of thousands of boys and girls have come of working age. They now form an army of unused youth. They must be an especial concern of democratic Government.

We must continue, above all things, to look for a solution of their special problem. For they, looking ahead to life, are entitled to action on our part and not merely to admonitions of optimism or lectures on economic laws.

Some in our midst have sought to instill a feeling of fear and defeatism in the minds of the American people about this problem.

To face the task of finding jobs faster than invention can take them away— is not defeatism. To warble easy platitudes that if we would only go back to ways that have failed, everything would be all right—is not courage.

In 1933 we met a problem of real fear and real defeatism. We faced the facts—with action and not with words alone.

The American people will reject the doctrine of fear, confident that in the 'thirties we have been building soundly a new order of things, different from the order of the 'twenties. In this dawn of the decade of the 'forties, with our program of social improvement started, we will continue to carry on the processes of recovery, so as to preserve our gains and provide jobs at living wages.

There are, of course, many other items of great public interest which could be enumerated in this message—the continued conservation of our natural resources, the improvement of health and of education, the extension of social security to larger groups, the freeing of large areas from restricted transportation discriminations, the extension of the merit system and many others.

Our continued progress in the social and economic field is important not only for the significance of each part of it but for the total effect which our program of domestic betterment has upon that most valuable asset of a nation in dangerous times—its national unity.

The permanent security of America in the present crisis does not lie in armed force alone. What we face is a set of world-wide forces of disintegration—vicious, ruthless, destructive of all the moral, religious and political standards which mankind, after centuries of struggle, has come to cherish most.

In these moral values, in these forces which have made our nation great, we must actively and practically reassert our faith.

These words—"national unity"—must not be allowed to be come merely a high-sounding phrase, a vague generality, a pious hope, to which everyone can give lip-service. They must be made to have real meaning in terms of the daily thoughts and acts of every man, woman and child in our land during the coming year and during the years that lie ahead.

For national unity is, in a very real and a very deep sense, the fundamental safeguard of all democracy.

Doctrines that set group against group, faith against faith, race against race, class against class, fanning the fires of hatred in men too despondent, too desperate to think for themselves, were used as rabble-rousing slogans on which dictators could ride to power. And once in power they could saddle their tyrannies on whole nations and on their weaker neighbors.

This is the danger to which we in America must begin to be more alert. For the apologists for foreign aggressors, and equally those selfish and partisan groups at home who wrap themselves in a false mantle of Americanism to promote their own economic, financial or political advantage, are now trying European tricks upon us, seeking to muddy the stream of our national thinking, weakening us in the face of danger, by trying to set our own people to fighting among themselves. Such tactics are what have helped to plunge Europe into war. We must combat them, as we would the plague, if American integrity and American security are to be preserved. We cannot afford to face the future as a disunited people.

We must as a united people keep ablaze on this continent the flames of human liberty, of reason, of democracy and of fair play as living things to be preserved for the better world that is to come.

Overstatement, bitterness, vituperation, and the beating of drums have contributed mightily to ill-feeling and wars between nations. If these unnecessary and unpleasant actions are harmful in the international field, if they have hurt in other parts of the world, they are also harmful in the domestic scene. Peace among ourselves would seem to have some of the advantage of peace between us and other nations. In the long run history amply demonstrates that angry controversy surely wins less than calm discussion.

In the spirit, therefore, of a greater unselfishness, recognizing that the world—including the United States of America—passes through perilous times, I am very hopeful that the closing session of the Seventy-sixth Congress will consider the needs of the nation and of humanity with calmness, with tolerance and with cooperative wisdom.

May the year 1940 be pointed to by our children as another period when democracy justified its existence as the best instrument of government yet devised by mankind.

State of the Union Address

Franklin D. Roosevelt

January 6, 1941

Mr. President, Mr. Speaker, Members of the Seventy-seventh Congress:

I address you, the Members of the Seventy-seventh Congress, at a moment unprecedented in the history of the Union. I use the word "unprecedented," because at no previous time has American security been as seriously threatened from without as it is today.

Since the permanent formation of our Government under the Constitution, in 1789, most of the periods of crisis in our history have related to our domestic affairs. Fortunately, only one of these—the four-year War Between the States—ever threatened our national unity. Today, thank God, one hundred and thirty million Americans, in forty-eight States, have forgotten points of the compass in our national unity.

It is true that prior to 1914 the United States often had been disturbed by events in other Continents. We had even engaged in two wars with European nations and in a number of undeclared wars in the West Indies, in the Mediterranean and in the Pacific for the maintenance of American rights and for the principles of peaceful commerce. But in no case had a serious threat been raised against our national safety or our continued independence.

What I seek to convey is the historic truth that the United States as a nation has at all times maintained clear, definite opposition, to any attempt to lock us in behind an ancient Chinese wall while the procession of civilization went past. Today, thinking of our children and of their children, we oppose enforced isolation for ourselves or for any other part of the Americas.

That determination of ours, extending over all these years, was proved, for example, during the quarter century of wars following the French Revolution.

While the Napoleonic struggles did threaten interests of the United States because of the French foothold in the West Indies and in Louisiana, and while we engaged in the War of 1812 to vindicate our right to peaceful trade, it is nevertheless clear that neither France nor Great Britain, nor any other nation, was aiming at domination of the whole world.

In like fashion from 1815 to 1914—ninety-nine years—no single war in Europe or in Asia constituted a real threat against our future or against the future of any other American nation.

Except in the Maximilian interlude in Mexico, no foreign power sought to establish itself in this Hemisphere; and the strength of the British fleet in the Atlantic has been a friendly strength. It is still a friendly strength.

Even when the World War broke out in 1914, it seemed to contain only small threat of danger to our own American future. But, as time went on, the American people began to visualize what the downfall of democratic nations might mean to our own democracy.

We need not overemphasize imperfections in the Peace of Versailles. We need not harp on failure of the democracies to deal with problems of world reconstruction. We should remember that the Peace of 1919 was far less unjust than the kind of "pacification" which began even before Munich, and which is being carried on under the new order of tyranny that seeks to spread over every continent today. The American people have unalterably set their faces against that tyranny.

Every realist knows that the democratic way of life is at this moment being directly assailed in every part of the world—assailed either by arms, or by secret spreading of poisonous propaganda by those who seek to destroy unity and promote discord in nations that are still at peace.

During sixteen long months this assault has blotted out the whole pattern of democratic life in an appalling number of independent nations, great and small. The assailants are still on the march, threatening other nations, great and small.

Therefore, as your President, performing my constitutional duty to "give to the Congress information of the state of the Union," I find it, unhappily, necessary to report that the future and the safety of our country and of our democracy are overwhelmingly involved in events far beyond our borders.

Armed defense of democratic existence is now being gallantly waged in four continents. If that defense fails, all the population and all the resources of Europe, Asia, Africa and Australasia will be dominated by the conquerors. Let us remember that the total of those populations and their resources in those four continents greatly exceeds the sum total of the population and the resources of the whole of the Western Hemisphere—many times over.

In times like these it is immature—and incidentally, untrue—for anybody to brag that an unprepared America, single-handed, and with one hand tied behind its back, can hold off the whole world.

No realistic American can expect from a dictator's peace international generosity, or return of true independence, or world disarmament, or freedom of expression, or freedom of religion—or even good business.

Such a peace would bring no security for us or for our neighbors. "Those, who would give up essential liberty to purchase a little temporary safety, deserve neither liberty nor safety."

As a nation, we may take pride in the fact that we are softhearted; but we cannot afford to be soft-headed.

We must always be wary of those who with sounding brass and a tinkling cymbal preach the "ism" of appeasement.

We must especially beware of that small group of selfish men who would clip the wings of the American eagle in order to feather their own nests.

I have recently pointed out how quickly the tempo of modern warfare could bring into our very midst the physical attack which we must eventually expect if the dictator nations win this war.

There is much loose talk of our immunity from immediate and direct invasion from across the seas. Obviously, as long as the British Navy retains its power, no such danger exists. Even if there were no British Navy, it is not probable that any enemy would be stupid enough to attack us by landing troops in the United States from across thousands of miles of ocean, until it had acquired strategic bases from which to operate.

But we learn much from the lessons of the past years in Europe—particularly the lesson of Norway, whose essential seaports were captured by treachery and surprise built up over a series of years.

The first phase of the invasion of this Hemisphere would not be the landing of regular troops. The necessary strategic points would be occupied by secret agents and their dupes—and great numbers of them are already here, and in Latin America.

As long as the aggressor nations maintain the offensive, they—not we—will choose the time and the place and the method of their attack.

That is why the future of all the American Republics is today in serious danger.

That is why this Annual Message to the Congress is unique in our history.

That is why every member of the Executive Branch of the Government and every member of the Congress faces great responsibility and great accountability.

The need of the moment is that our actions and our policy should be devoted primarily—almost exclusively—to meeting this foreign peril. For all our domestic problems are now a part of the great emergency.

Just as our national policy in internal affairs has been based upon a decent respect for the rights and the dignity of all our fellow men within our gates, so our national policy in foreign affairs has been based on a decent respect for the rights and dignity of all nations, large and small. And the justice of morality must and will win in the end.

Our national policy is this:

First, by an impressive expression of the public will and without regard to partisanship, we are committed to all-inclusive national defense.

Second, by an impressive expression of the public will and without regard to partisanship, we are committed to full support of all those resolute peoples, everywhere, who are resisting aggression and are thereby keeping war away from our Hemisphere. By this support, we express our determination that the democratic cause shall prevail; and we strengthen the defense and the security of our own nation.

Third, by an impressive expression of the public will and without regard to partisanship, we are committed to the proposition that principles of morality and considerations for our own security will never permit us to acquiesce in a peace dictated by aggressors and sponsored by appeasers. We know that enduring peace cannot be bought at the cost of other people's freedom.

In the recent national election there was no substantial difference between the two great parties in respect to that national policy. No issue was fought out on this line before the American electorate. Today it is abundantly evident that American citizens everywhere are demanding and supporting speedy and complete action in recognition of obvious danger.

Therefore, the immediate need is a swift and driving increase in our armament production.

Leaders of industry and labor have responded to our summons. Goals of speed have been set. In some cases these goals are being reached ahead of time; in some cases we are on schedule; in other cases there are slight but not serious delays; and in some cases—and I am sorry to say very important cases—we are all concerned by the slowness of the accomplishment of our plans.

The Army and Navy, however, have made substantial progress during the past year. Actual experience is improving and speeding up our methods of production with every passing day. And today's best is not good enough for tomorrow.

I am not satisfied with the progress thus far made. The men in charge of the program represent the best in training, in ability, and in patriotism. They are not satisfied with the progress thus far made. None of us will be satisfied until the job is done.

No matter whether the original goal was set too high or too low, our objective is quicker and better results. To give you two illustrations:

We are behind schedule in turning out finished airplanes; we are working day and night to solve the innumerable problems and to catch up.

We are ahead of schedule in building warships but we are working to get even further ahead of that schedule.

To change a whole nation from a basis of peacetime production of implements of peace to a basis of wartime production of implements of war is no small task. And the greatest difficulty comes at the beginning of the program, when new tools, new plant facilities, new assembly lines, and new ship ways must first be constructed before the actual materiel begins to flow steadily and speedily from them.

The Congress, of course, must rightly keep itself informed at all times of the progress of the program. However, there is certain information, as the Congress itself will readily recognize, which, in the interests of our own security and those of the nations that we are supporting, must of needs be kept in confidence.

New circumstances are constantly begetting new needs for our safety. I shall ask this Congress for greatly increased new appropriations and authorizations to carry on what we have begun.

I also ask this Congress for authority and for funds sufficient to manufacture additional munitions and war supplies of many kinds, to be turned over to those nations which are now in actual war with aggressor nations.

Our most useful and immediate role is to act as an arsenal for them as well as for ourselves. They do not need man power, but they do need billions of dollars worth of the weapons of defense.

The time is near when they will not be able to pay for them all in ready cash. We cannot, and we will not, tell them that they must surrender, merely because of present inability to pay for the weapons which we know they must have.

I do not recommend that we make them a loan of dollars with which to pay for these weapons—a loan to be repaid in dollars.

I recommend that we make it possible for those nations to continue to obtain war materials in the United States, fitting their orders into our own program. Nearly all their materiel would, if the time ever came, be useful for our own defense.

Taking counsel of expert military and naval authorities, considering what is best for our own security, we are free to decide how much should be kept here and how much should be sent abroad to our friends who by their determined and heroic resistance are giving us time in which to make ready our own defense.

For what we send abroad, we shall be repaid within a reasonable time following the close of hostilities, in similar materials, or, at our option, in other goods of many kinds, which they can produce and which we need.

Let us say to the democracies: "We Americans are vitally concerned in your defense of freedom. We are putting forth our energies, our resources and our organizing powers to give you the strength to regain and maintain a free world. We shall send you, in ever-increasing numbers, ships, planes, tanks, guns. This is our purpose and our pledge."

In fulfillment of this purpose we will not be intimidated by the threats of dictators that they will regard as a breach of international law or as an act of war our aid to the democracies which dare to resist their aggression. Such aid is not an act of war, even if a dictator should unilaterally proclaim it so to be.

When the dictators, if the dictators, are ready to make war upon us, they will not wait for an act of war on our part. They did not wait for Norway or Belgium or the Netherlands to commit an act of war.

Their only interest is in a new one-way international law, which lacks mutuality in its observance, and, therefore, becomes an instrument of oppression.

The happiness of future generations of Americans may well depend upon how effective and how immediate we can make our aid felt. No one can tell the exact character of the emergency situations that we may be called upon to meet. The Nation's hands must not be tied when the Nation's life is in danger.

We must all prepare to make the sacrifices that the emergency—almost as serious as war itself—demands. Whatever stands in the way of speed and efficiency in defense preparations must give way to the national need.

A free nation has the right to expect full cooperation from all groups. A free nation has the right to look to the leaders of business, of labor, and of agriculture to take the lead in stimulating effort, not among other groups but within their own groups.

The best way of dealing with the few slackers or trouble makers in our midst is, first, to shame them by patriotic example, and, if that fails, to use the sovereignty of Government to save Government.

As men do not live by bread alone, they do not fight by armaments alone. Those who man our defenses, and those behind them who build our defenses, must have the stamina and the courage which come from unshakable belief in the manner of life which they are defending. The mighty action that we are calling for cannot be based on a disregard of all things worth fighting for.

The Nation takes great satisfaction and much strength from the things which have been done to make its people conscious of their individual stake in the preservation of democratic life in America. Those things have toughened the fibre of our people, have renewed their faith and strengthened their devotion to the institutions we make ready to protect.

Certainly this is no time for any of us to stop thinking about the social and economic problems which are the root cause of the social revolution which is today a supreme factor in the world.

For there is nothing mysterious about the foundations of a healthy and strong democracy. The basic things expected by our people of their political and economic systems are simple. They are:

Equality of opportunity for youth and for others.

Jobs for those who can work.

Security for those who need it.

The ending of special privilege for the few.

The preservation of civil liberties for all.

The enjoyment of the fruits of scientific progress in a wider and constantly rising standard of living.

These are the simple, basic things that must never be lost sight of in the turmoil and unbelievable complexity of our modern world. The inner and abiding strength of our economic and political systems is dependent upon the degree to which they fulfill these expectations.

Many subjects connected with our social economy call for immediate improvement.

As examples:

We should bring more citizens under the coverage of old-age pensions and unemployment insurance.

We should widen the opportunities for adequate medical care.

We should plan a better system by which persons deserving or needing gainful employment may obtain it.

I have called for personal sacrifice. I am assured of the willingness of almost all Americans to respond to that call.

A part of the sacrifice means the payment of more money in taxes. In my Budget Message I shall recommend that a greater portion of this great defense program be paid for from taxation than we are paying today. No person should try, or be allowed, to get rich out of this program; and the principle of tax payments in accordance with ability to pay should be constantly before our eyes to guide our legislation.

If the Congress maintains these principles, the voters, putting patriotism ahead of pocketbooks, will give you their applause.

In the future days, which we seek to make secure, we look forward to a world founded upon four essential human freedoms.

The first is freedom of speech and expression—everywhere in the world.

The second is freedom of every person to worship God in his own way—everywhere in the world.

The third is freedom from want—which, translated into world terms, means economic understandings which will secure to every nation a healthy peacetime life for its inhabitants—everywhere in the world.

The fourth is freedom from fear—which, translated into world terms, means a world-wide reduction of armaments to such a point and in such a thorough fashion that no nation will be in a position to commit an act of physical aggression against any neighbor—anywhere in the world.

That is no vision of a distant millennium. It is a definite basis for a kind of world attainable in our own time and generation. That kind of world is the very antithesis of the so-called new order of tyranny which the dictators seek to create with the crash of a bomb.

To that new order we oppose the greater conception—the moral order. A good society is able to face schemes of world domination and foreign revolutions alike without fear.

Since the beginning of our American history, we have been engaged in change—in a perpetual peaceful revolution—a revolution which goes on steadily, quietly adjusting itself to changing conditions—without the concentration camp or the quick-lime in the ditch. The world order which we seek is the cooperation of free countries, working together in a friendly, civilized society.

This nation has placed its destiny in the hands and heads and hearts of its millions of free men and women; and its faith in freedom under the guidance of God. Freedom means the supremacy of human rights everywhere. Our support goes to those who struggle to gain those rights or keep them. Our strength is our unity of purpose. To that high concept there can be no end save victory.

State of the Union Address

Franklin D. Roosevelt

January 6, 1942

In fulfilling my duty to report upon the State of the Union, I am proud to say to you that the spirit of the American people was never higher than it is today—the Union was never more closely knit together—this country was never more deeply determined to face the solemn tasks before it.

The response of the American people has been instantaneous, and it will be sustained until our security is assured.

Exactly one year ago today I said to this Congress: "When the dictators. . . are ready to make war upon us, they will not wait for an act of war on our part. . . . They—not we—will choose the time and the place and the method of their attack."

We now know their choice of the time: a peaceful Sunday morning—December 7, 1941.

We know their choice of the place: an American outpost in the Pacific.

We know their choice of the method: the method of Hitler himself.

Japan's scheme of conquest goes back half a century. It was not merely a policy of seeking living room: it was a plan which included the subjugation of all the peoples in the Far East and in the islands of the Pacific, and the domination of that ocean by Japanese military and naval control of the western coasts of North, Central, and South America.

The development of this ambitious conspiracy was marked by the war against China in 1894; the subsequent occupation of Korea; the war against Russia in 1904; the illegal fortification of the mandated Pacific islands following 1920; the seizure of Manchuria in 1931; and the invasion of China in 1937.

A similar policy of criminal conquest was adopted by Italy. The Fascists first revealed their imperial designs in Libya and Tripoli. In 1935 they seized Abyssinia. Their goal was the domination of all North Africa, Egypt, parts of France, and the entire Mediterranean world.

But the dreams of empire of the Japanese and Fascist leaders were modest in comparison with the gargantuan aspirations of Hitler and his Nazis. Even before they came to power in 1933, their plans for that conquest had been drawn. Those plans provided for ultimate domination, not of any one section of the world, but of the whole earth and all the oceans on it.

When Hitler organized his Berlin-Rome-Tokyo alliance, all these plans of conquest became a single plan. Under this, in addition to her own schemes of conquest, Japan's role was obviously to cut off our supply of weapons of war to Britain, and Russia and China—weapons which increasingly were speeding the day of Hitler's doom. The act of Japan at Pearl Harbor was intended to stun us—to terrify us to such an extent that we would divert our industrial and military strength to the Pacific area, or even to our own continental defense.

The plan has failed in its purpose. We have not been stunned. We have not been terrified or confused. This very reassembling of the Seventy-seventh Congress today is proof of that; for the mood of quiet, grim resolution which here prevails bodes ill for those who conspired and collaborated to murder world peace.

That mood is stronger than any mere desire for revenge. It expresses the will of the American people to make very certain that the world will never so suffer again.

Admittedly, we have been faced with hard choices. It was bitter, for example, not to be able to relieve the heroic and historic defenders of Wake Island. It was bitter for us not to be able to land a million men in a thousand ships in the Philippine Islands.

But this adds only to our determination to see to it that the Stars and Stripes will fly again over Wake and Guam. Yes, see to it that the brave people of the Philippines will be rid of Japanese imperialism; and will live in freedom, security, and independence.

Powerful and offensive actions must and will be taken in proper time. The consolidation of the United Nations' total war effort against our common enemies is being achieved.

That was and is the purpose of conferences which have been held during the past two weeks in Washington, and Moscow and Chungking. That is the primary objective of the declaration of solidarity signed in Washington on January 1, 1942, by 26 Nations united against the Axis powers.

Difficult choices may have to be made in the months to come. We do not shrink from such decisions. We and those united with us will make those decisions with courage and determination.

Plans have been laid here and in the other capitals for coordinated and cooperative action by all the United Nations—military action and economic action. Already we have established, as you know, unified command of land, sea, and air forces in the southwestern Pacific theater of war. There will be a continuation of conferences and consultations among military staffs, so that the plans and operations of each will fit into the general strategy designed to crush the enemy. We shall not fight isolated wars—each Nation going its own way. These 26 Nations are united—not in spirit and determination alone, but in the broad conduct of the war in all its phases.

For the first time since the Japanese and the Fascists and the Nazis started along their blood-stained course of conquest they now face the fact that superior forces are assembling against them. Gone forever are the days when the aggressors could attack and destroy their victims one by one without unity of resistance. We of the United Nations will so dispose our forces that we can strike at the common enemy wherever the greatest damage can be done him.

The militarists of Berlin and Tokyo started this war. But the massed, angered forces of common humanity will finish it.

Destruction of the material and spiritual centers of civilization—this has been and still is the purpose of Hitler and his Italian and Japanese chessmen.

They would wreck the power of the British Commonwealth and Russia and China and the Netherlands—and then combine all their forces to achieve their ultimate goal, the conquest of the United States.

They know that victory for us means victory for freedom.

They know that victory for us means victory for the institution of democracy—the ideal of the family, the simple principles of common decency and humanity.

They know that victory for us means victory for religion. And they could not tolerate that. The world is too small to provide adequate "living room" for both Hitler and God. In proof of that, the Nazis have now announced their plan for enforcing their new German, pagan religion all over the world—a plan by which the Holy Bible and the Cross of Mercy would be displaced by Mein Kampf and the swastika and the naked sword.

Our own objectives are clear; the objective of smashing the militarism imposed by war lords upon their enslaved peoples the objective of liberating the subjugated Nations—the objective of establishing and securing freedom of speech, freedom of religion, freedom from want, and freedom from fear everywhere in the world.

We shall not stop short of these objectives—nor shall we be satisfied merely to gain them and then call it a day. I know that I speak for the American people—and I have good reason to believe that I speak also for all the other peoples who fight with us—when I say that this time we are determined not only to win the war, but also to maintain the security of the peace that will follow.

But we know that modern methods of warfare make it a task, not only of shooting and fighting, but an even more urgent one of working and producing.

Victory requires the actual weapons of war and the means of transporting them to a dozen points of combat.

It will not be sufficient for us and the other United Nations to produce a slightly superior supply of munitions to that of Germany, Japan, Italy, and the stolen industries in the countries which they have overrun.

The superiority of the United Nations in munitions and ships must be overwhelming—so overwhelming that the Axis Nations can never hope to catch up with it. And so, in order to attain this overwhelming superiority the United States must build planes and tanks and guns and ships to the utmost limit of our national capacity. We have the ability and capacity to produce arms not only for our own forces, but also for the armies, navies, and air forces fighting on our side.

And our overwhelming superiority of armament must be adequate to put weapons of war at the proper time into the hands of those men in the conquered Nations who stand ready to seize the first opportunity to revolt against their German and Japanese oppressors, and against the traitors in their own ranks, known by the already infamous name of "Quislings." And I think that it is a fair prophecy to say that, as we get guns to the patriots in those lands, they too will fire shots heard 'round the world.

This production of ours in the United States must be raised far above present levels, even though it will mean the dislocation of the lives and occupations of millions of our own people. We must raise our sights all along the production line. Let no man say it cannot be done. It must be done—and we have undertaken to do it.

I have just sent a letter of directive to the appropriate departments and agencies of our Government, ordering that immediate steps be taken:

First, to increase our production rate of airplanes so rapidly that in this year, 1942, we shall produce 60,000 planes, 10,000 more than the goal that we set a year and a half ago. This includes 45,000 combat planes—bombers, dive bombers, pursuit planes. The rate of increase will be maintained and continued so that next year, 1943, we shall produce 125,000 airplanes, including 100,000 combat planes.

Second, to increase our production rate of tanks so rapidly that in this year, 1942, we shall produce 45,000 tanks; and to continue that increase so that next year, 1943, we shall produce 75,000 tanks.

Third, to increase our production rate of anti-aircraft guns so rapidly that in this year, 1942, we shall produce 20,000 of them; and to continue that increase so that next year, 1943, we shall produce 35,000 anti-aircraft guns.

And fourth, to increase our production rate of merchant ships so rapidly that in this year, 1942, we shall build 6,000,000 deadweight tons as compared with a 1941 completed production of 1,100,000. And finally, we shall continue that increase so that next year, 1943, we shall build 10,000,000 tons of shipping.

These figures and similar figures for a multitude of other implements of war will give the Japanese and the Nazis a little idea of just what they accomplished in the attack at Pearl Harbor.

And I rather hope that all these figures which I have given will become common knowledge in Germany and Japan.

Our task is hard—our task is unprecedented—and the time is short. We must strain every existing armament-producing facility to the utmost. We must convert every available plant and tool to war production. That goes all the way from the greatest plants to the smallest—from the huge automobile industry to the village machine shop.

Production for war is based on men and women—the human hands and brains which collectively we call Labor. Our workers stand ready to work long hours; to turn out more in a day's work; to keep the wheels turning and the fires burning twenty-four hours a day, and seven days a week. They realize well that on the speed and efficiency of their work depend the lives of their sons and their brothers on the fighting fronts.

Production for war is based on metals and raw materials—steel, copper, rubber, aluminum, zinc, tin. Greater and greater quantities of them will have to be diverted to war purposes. Civilian use of them will have to be cut further and still further—and, in many cases, completely eliminated.

War costs money. So far, we have hardly even begun to pay for it. We have devoted only 15 percent of our national income to national defense. As will appear in my Budget Message tomorrow, our war program for the coming fiscal year will cost 56 billion dollars or, in other words, more than half of the estimated annual national income. That means taxes and bonds and bonds and taxes. It means cutting luxuries and other non-essentials. In a word, it means an "all-out" war by individual effort and family effort in a united country.

Only this all-out scale of production will hasten the ultimate all-out victory. Speed will count. Lost ground can always be regained—lost time never. Speed will save lives; speed will save this Nation which is in peril; speed will save our freedom and our civilization—and slowness has never been an American characteristic.

As the United States goes into its full stride, we must always be on guard against misconceptions which will arise, some of them naturally, or which will be planted among us by our enemies.

We must guard against complacency. We must not underrate the enemy. He is powerful and cunning—and cruel and ruthless. He will stop at nothing that gives him a chance to kill and to destroy. He has trained his people to believe that their highest perfection is achieved by waging war. For many years he has prepared for this very conflict—planning, and plotting, and training, arming, and fighting. We have already tasted defeat. We may suffer further setbacks. We must face the fact of a hard war, a long war, a bloody war, a costly war.

We must, on the other hand, guard against defeatism. That has been one of the chief weapons of Hitler's propaganda machine—used time and again with deadly results. It will not be used successfully on the American people.

We must guard against divisions among ourselves and among all the other United Nations. We must be particularly vigilant against racial discrimination in any of its ugly forms. Hitler will try again to breed mistrust and suspicion between one individual and another, one group and another, one race and another, one Government and another. He will try to use the same technique of falsehood and rumor-mongering with which he divided France from Britain. He is trying to do this with us even now. But he will find a unity of will and purpose against him, which will persevere until the destruction of all his black designs upon the freedom and safety of the people of the world.

We cannot wage this war in a defensive spirit. As our power and our resources are fully mobilized, we shall carry the attack against the enemy—we shall hit him and hit him again wherever and whenever we can reach him.

We must keep him far from our shores, for we intend to bring this battle to him on his own home grounds.

American armed forces must be used at any place in all the world where it seems advisable to engage the forces of the enemy. In some cases these operations will be defensive, in order to protect key positions. In other cases, these operations will be offensive, in order to strike at the common enemy, with a view to his complete encirclement and eventual total defeat.

American armed forces will operate at many points in the Far East.

American armed forces will be on all the oceans—helping to guard the essential communications which are vital to the United Nations.

American land and air and sea forces will take stations in the British Isles—which constitute an essential fortress in this great world struggle.

American armed forces will help to protect this hemisphere—and also help to protect bases outside this hemisphere, which could be used for an attack on the Americas.

If any of our enemies, from Europe or from Asia, attempt long-range raids by "suicide" squadrons of bombing planes, they will do so only in the hope of terrorizing our people and disrupting our morale. Our people are not afraid of that. We know that we may have to pay a heavy price for freedom. We will pay this price with a will. Whatever the price, it is a thousand times worth it. No matter what our enemies, in their desperation, may attempt to do to us—we will say, as the people of London have said, "We can take it." And what's more we can give it back and we will give it back—with compound interest.

When our enemies challenged our country to stand up and fight, they challenged each and every one of us. And each and every one of us has accepted the challenge—for himself and for his Nation.

There were only some 400 United States Marines who in the heroic and historic defense of Wake Island inflicted such great losses on the enemy. Some of those men were killed in action; and others are now prisoners of war. When the survivors of that great fight are liberated and restored to their homes, they will learn that a hundred and thirty million of their fellow citizens have been inspired to render their own full share of service and sacrifice.

We can well say that our men on the fighting fronts have already proved that Americans today are just as rugged and just as tough as any of the heroes whose exploits we celebrate on the Fourth of July.

Many people ask, "When will this war end?" There is only one answer to that. It will end just as soon as we make it end, by our combined efforts, our combined strength, our combined determination to fight through and work through until the end—the end of militarism in Germany and Italy and Japan. Most certainly we shall not settle for less.

That is the spirit in which discussions have been conducted during the visit of the British Prime Minister to Washington. Mr. Churchill and I understand each other, our motives and our purposes. Together, during the past two weeks, we have faced squarely the major military and economic problems of this greatest world war.

All in our Nation have been cheered by Mr. Churchill's visit. We have been deeply stirred by his great message to us. He is welcome in our midst, and we unite in wishing him a safe return to his home.

For we are fighting on the same side with the British people, who fought alone for long, terrible months, and withstood the enemy with fortitude and tenacity and skill.

We are fighting on the same side with the Russian people who have seen the Nazi hordes swarm up to the very gates of Moscow, and who with almost superhuman will and courage have forced the invaders back into retreat.

We are fighting on the same side as the brave people of China—those millions who for four and a half long years have withstood bombs and starvation and have whipped the invaders time and again in spite of the superior Japanese equipment and arms. Yes, we are fighting on the same side as the indomitable Dutch. We are fighting on the same side as all the other Governments in exile, whom Hitler and all his armies and all his Gestapo have not been able to conquer.

But we of the United Nations are not making all this sacrifice of human effort and human lives to return to the kind of world we had after the last world war.

We are fighting today for security, for progress, and for peace, not only for ourselves but for all men, not only for one generation but for all generations. We are fighting to cleanse the world of ancient evils, ancient ills.

Our enemies are guided by brutal cynicism, by unholy contempt for the human race. We are inspired by a faith that goes back through all the years to the first chapter of the Book of Genesis: "God created man in His own image."

We on our side are striving to be true to that divine heritage. We are fighting, as our fathers have fought, to uphold the doctrine that all men are equal in the sight of God. Those on the other side are striving to destroy this deep belief and to create a world in their own image—a world of tyranny and cruelty and serfdom.

That is the conflict that day and night now pervades our lives.

No compromise can end that conflict. There never has been—there never can be—successful compromise between good and evil. Only total victory can reward the champions of tolerance, and decency, and freedom, and faith.

Echo Library
www.echo-library.com

Echo Library uses advanced digital print-on-demand technology to build and preserve an exciting world class collection of rare and out-of-print books, making them readily available for everyone to enjoy.

Situated just yards from Teddington Lock on the River Thames, Echo Library was founded in 2005 by Tom Cherrington, a specialist dealer in rare and antiquarian books with a passion for literature.

Please visit our website for a complete catalogue of our books, which includes foreign language titles.

The Right to Read

Echo Library actively supports the Royal National Institute of the Blind's Right to Read initiative by publishing a comprehensive range of large print and clear print titles.

Large Print titles are in 16 point Tiresias font as recommended by the RNIB.

Clear Print titles are in 13 point Tiresias font and designed for those who find standard print difficult to read.

Customer Service

If there is a serious error in the text or layout please send details to feedback@echo-library.com and we will supply a corrected copy. If there is a printing fault or the book is damaged please refer to your supplier.

Breinigsville, PA USA
11 July 2010
241543BV00001B/117/A